"Prepares congregational leaders with the faithful courage required for today's church."
—**Rev. David Schoen**, minister and team leader, Congregational Assessment, Support and Advancement, United Church of Christ

"Visionary and engaging ways to navigate … change and conflict. This accessible, practical, intelligent, disarmingly honest book will be one I reach for often."
—**Rev. Dr. Lucy A. Forster-Smith**, author, *College & University Chaplaincy in the 21st Century: A Multifaith Look at the Practice of Ministry on Campuses across America*

"Brings calm clarity to the turbulent topic of conflict that congregations struggle with…. A welcome and hopeful message."
—**Rev. Laurie Miller Vischer**, associate pastor, Westminster Presbyterian Church, Portland, Oregon

"With spiritual sensitivity, affection and respect for congregational life … offers important approaches to change and conflict that are resourceful, creatively imaginative and life-giving. Goes beyond a 'how-to' to become a compelling read."
—**Rev. Dr. Barbara T. Cheney**, missional pastor, St. James Episcopal Church, New Haven, Connecticut

"Faithful, honest and hopeful…. A well-written, deeply informed source of solid advice based on hard-won experience, a gift to anyone who shares her love for communities of faith."
—**Rev. LeDayne McLeese Polaski**, executive director, Bautistas por la Paz (Baptist Peace Fellowship)

"I wish my church would read this book. Immediately. Twice. And no churchgoer needs to read it more than I do…. A calm, plainspoken, practical guide."
—**John Backman**, author, *Why Can't We Talk? Christian Wisdom on Dialogue as a Habit of the Heart*

"Where was this book when I started out in ministry?… More than a self-help book for congregations to navigate through their challenges—this is a theologically based, vision-centered approach to transform leadership toward gospel service."
—**David Haas**, liturgical composer; director, Emmaus Center for Music, Prayer and Ministry; campus minister, Cretin-Derham Hall, St. Paul, Minnesota; director, Music Ministry Alive!

"Provides pathways for reconciliation that are universal. Bradshaw's years of experience with conflict management in congregations were comforting and strengthening; I felt I was in good hands."
—**Rev. Meg Riley**, senior minister, Church of the Larger Fellowship (UU), Boston

"Anita Bradshaw has done it! As a thoroughly engaging storyteller, she's written an amazingly accessible guide for your congregation's pilgrimage through inevitable change and conflict."
—**Rev. Dr. Gary M. Simpson**, Northwestern Lutheran Theological Seminary Chair in Theology, Luther Seminary

CHANGE &
CONFLICT
IN YOUR
CONGREGATION
(Even If You Hate Both)

How to Implement
Conscious Choices,
Manage Emotions &
Build a Thriving
Christian Community

REV. ANITA L. BRADSHAW, PhD

CHRISTIAN JOURNEYS
FROM SKYLIGHT PATHS® PUBLISHING
Woodstock, Vermont

Change and Conflict in Your Congregation (Even If You Hate Both):
How to Implement Conscious Choices, Manage Emotions and Build a Thriving Christian Community
2015 Quality Paperback Edition, First Printing
© 2015 by Anita L. Bradshaw

For information regarding permission to reprint material from this book, please mail or fax your request in writing to SkyLight Paths Publishing, Permissions Department, at the address / fax number listed below, or email your request to permissions@skylightpaths.com.

Unless otherwise noted, all biblical quotations are from the New Revised Standard Version (Anglicized Edition), © 1989, 1995 by the Division of Christian Education of the National Council of the Churches of Christ in the United States of America. Used by permission. All rights reserved.

"What Is a Next Level Church?" graph used by permission of the Center for Progressive Renewal.

Library of Congress Cataloging-in-Publication Data
Bradshaw, Anita L., 1957–
Change and conflict in your congregation (even if you hate both) : how to implement conscious choices, manage emotions, and build a thriving Christian community / Rev. Anita L. Bradshaw, PhD.
     pages cm
Includes bibliographical references.
ISBN 978-1-59473-578-3 (quality pbk.) — ISBN 978-1-59473-595-0 (ebook) 1. Church management. 2. Change—Religious aspects—Christianity. 3. Conflict management—Religious aspects—Christianity I. Title.
BV652.B65 2015
254—dc23
                              2014046004
10 9 8 7 6 5 4 3 2 1
Manufactured in the United States of America
Cover design: Jenny Buono
Cover art: © happydancing / Shutterstock
Interior design: Tim Holtz

SkyLight Paths Publishing is creating a place where people of different spiritual traditions come together for challenge and inspiration, a place where we can help each other understand the mystery that lies at the heart of our existence.

SkyLight Paths sees both believers and seekers as a community that increasingly transcends traditional boundaries of religion and denomination—people wanting to learn from each other, *walking together, finding the way.*

SkyLight Paths, "Walking Together, Finding the Way" and colophon are trademarks of Long-Hill Partners, Inc., registered in the U.S. Patent and Trademark Office.

Walking Together, Finding the Way®
Published by SkyLight Paths Publishing
A Division of LongHill Partners, Inc.
Sunset Farm Offices, Route 4, P.O. Box 237
Woodstock, VT 05091
Tel: (802) 457-4000 Fax: (802) 457-4004
www.skylightpaths.com

Contents

Acknowledgments

I owe a great deal of thanks to many people and congregations I have known and served over the years. I offer thanks to:

- All of the congregations I have served and worked with. You have taught me much and I hope only that what I gave in return was a blessing to you.
- My teachers and mentors: Margaret Farley, the late Letty Russell, Mary Hess, Gary Simpson, Richard Blackburn, Patrick Keifert, Pat Taylor Ellison, and the consultants and staff at Church Innovations Institute. What I have learned from all these individuals is reflected throughout the book and in my work.
- David Haas, for cajoling me many years ago to write.
- Many colleagues and friends who have taught me much and encouraged me: Cameron Trimble and Michael Piazza of the Center for Progressive Renewal, David Schoen, and Sarah Campbell.
- My online writing group and coach from Academic Writing Club: MLC, mtrex, and KarenR. Without these three women, this book would probably still be languishing in the recesses of my brain.
- My "Visions Group": Jen, Doug, Joan, Chris, and Liz, as well as Tom. You have cheered me on in so many ways to realize this dream and vision for my life.
- The late Rev. Dr. Don Hadfield, who believed in me and always encouraged me to keep going.
- My editor, Emily Wichland, who sought me out and suggested this book. You have been kind, patient, and encouraging, and I hope we work together for many years.
- And finally, to Sherrie, my rock and my love. You make all worthwhile.

Introduction

The first three congregations I belonged to after seminary, either as a member or on staff, were all in extreme conflict. I wondered at one point if this was any reflection on me. I decided it was not—but it was hard not to take it personally, especially when people *made* it personal and some of that ugliness got directed toward me.

My skin is thicker now, but my gut still can get into a mighty uproar when people in the church get nasty. I suppose it is naiveté on my part, but I still expect Christians to act . . . well, like Christians. I grew up singing that folk hymn "They Will Know We Are Christians by Our Love." And frankly, there are days that love is not in evidence. Love has been often missing in our congregations, and we wonder why the world is not interested in joining us.

I also know a great deal more now than I did those many years ago when I was caught in the turmoil and chaos of those first three congregations. But when I reflect back on my experiences, I am surprised I didn't make more mistakes and, in some ways, surprised that I am still in ministry. I want to offer encouragement and guidance to you in the hopes that you can avoid some of my mistakes and will have tools to deal with the situations you face.

Each congregation's conflict was unique, and yet they shared many characteristics. The conflicts were rooted in pastoral misconduct, a pastor's alcoholism, a small group of "old guard" members bullying and holding the congregation hostage, and a tiny circle of people working to undermine the pastors. The behaviors exhibited were fairly common in congregational conflict: a divide-and-conquer strategy; bullying; secret meetings; petitions meant to split the congregation; a few speaking for many (as in, "lots of us think"); dissemination of false information, rumors, and innuendo; and a host of other less than Christian behaviors. I wouldn't say I saw it *all* in those years after seminary, but I saw a *lot* of the ugly underside of church. Such stuff is not for the faint of heart.

Charting Our Way Through Conflict and Change

This book is a result of what I learned in those churches—and in many others since in my ministry as a pastor, consultant, and denominational leader. I finally figured out that although heart-rending conflict was the state of the church or many churches, it didn't have to be so. It is possible to be church in a way that doesn't involve ugliness, even if it involves conflict.

The church is always going to see conflict, especially when things change—and things are always changing, internally and externally, for the church. And if many congregations in the mainline Protestant denominations are going to survive, much less thrive, those churches are going to need to change a lot to move into a new day.

Change is something that tends to "happen" in congregations. There are things that happen that we cannot anticipate. Yet many changes could be planned and intentionally implemented, if leaders really wanted to do so. Why are the processes of change and conflict in congregations often resisted, ignored, or treated as if they are totally abnormal?

Conflicts are an opportunity for the community of faith to grow deeper into the reality that the church is called to be a reconciling community. In this book I hope to provide you with some practical methods of conflict resolution and change management to facilitate such growth.

The first chapter focuses on the reasons conflict and change are unwelcome in churches. Congregational leaders need to understand these reasons in order to address them, resolve conflict, and bring about necessary changes to move beyond conflict and re-engage with the mission of the church. Church leaders and members generally see conflict itself as a negative in the church, instead of recognizing that the problem is the bad behaviors that result from conflict. Conflict can be managed, but it often isn't. The most common reaction to conflict is to try to ignore it and hope and pray it goes away. But it never does. It may go underground, but it will not go away until it is resolved.

The second chapter moves from reasons for resistance to a new way of viewing change and conflict in congregations. If our attitude is always that conflict is negative or scary, we will have a difficult time working with it and learning how to use conflict for good in the midst of change. Congregations can deal differently with both conflict and change, but we must make a conscious choice to do so. And usually the choice is stronger if it is an educated one, because it is really a choice to develop a positive theology of change and conflict. I offer several building blocks for developing such a positive theology.

The first of these building blocks is the Bible. The stories and teachings in the Bible assume that conflict and change are a natural and normal part of individual and community life. Rooted in both our finitude and our sinfulness, conflict is bound to arise. We must be clear that conflict is not sinful in and of itself. We definitely see sinful reactions and behaviors arising out of conflict, but conflict is not sinful.

The second building block is from the history of the Christian church. Typically non-Catholic and non-Orthodox Christians are called Protestants, and we forget the root of that name is *protest*. But our common history, Protestant or not, is one of conflict. Throughout history the church has dealt with debates, protests, and change after change, internally and externally.

A third building block is in our understanding of the work of the Holy Spirit and of what the church is. Our theological approach to conflict and change can give us room to see both as not only natural and normal, but also as the work of the Holy Spirit within the community of faith.

> It is possible to be church in a way that doesn't involve ugliness, even if it involves conflict.

Chapter 3 examines the process of change and offers strategies for managing it. There is a wealth of literature and theories on change and change management. This chapter draws from two of those theories—Ronald A. Heifetz's work on technical and adaptive change and Everett M. Rogers's *Diffusion of Innovations*. These scholars offer complementary ways of viewing change that lend themselves to specific strategies for managing the process and minimizing the potential for conflict to arise from it.

The fourth chapter focuses on strategies for working with and thriving through conflict. We don't need to like conflict to find ways to see it as useful and helpful. Conflict is not either present or absent. We experience varying degrees of conflict, and each degree requires a different strategy to address it. In addition, church leaders (clergy and lay) must be aware of our own reactions to conflict and manage our own anxiety, as well as that of the congregation. I have observed some conflicts that arise due to the anxiety of the leaders. If leaders are anxious and ratchet up the anxiety in the congregation, conflict will erupt even though we are trying to keep it from doing so. Being a nonanxious presence is essential for leaders, as is establishing clear boundaries around appropriate and inappropriate behavior within a community of faith. This chapter covers some methods for handling extreme behaviors and using the energy around conflict to move a congregation forward.

Chapter 5 takes up the dualistic thinking that prevails in both our society and our congregations. We tend to see things in terms of either/or, especially in times of tension. This chapter takes on this phenomenon of extremes and suggests ways to manage the polarities that often underlie them. Polarities that develop in the midst of conflict and change can divide congregations and inhibit our ability to think imaginatively about the situations we face and possible responses to them. Learning to manage polarities is a critical skill for leaders in congregations, and once we attempt this, we may find that the most creative responses begin to emerge.

> We don't need to like conflict to find ways to see it as useful and helpful.

A key to resisting dualistic thinking is exercising imagination, and this chapter explores the matter. It also examines the life cycle of congregations and how imagination or lack of imagination comes into play at various stages. You'll find some helpful (and fun!) strategies for reviving imagination in this chapter.

Finally, chapter 6 looks at the importance of story in the life of a congregation and the effect of these narratives on building a future. Congregations, as well as individuals, create stories to explain who and what we are. These stories often have some dimension of truth, but many times they reflect interpretations of the truth that are unhelpful as a congregation tries to move into the future. This chapter proposes ways we can change the story to lead us into a future that reflects who we truly are and what God is calling the congregation to be.

Understanding the Church as an Organization

Organizations, like individuals, are often resistant to change. To address change takes energy, and it often requires further changes in a congregation's system, structure, policies, procedures, even bylaws and constitutions. It also takes time. Churches often seek input from everyone for every change or decision. While seeking input and opinions is vital, it is simply not wise to expect that everyone will buy into every change. Waiting for input and approval can cause congregations to take an inordinate amount of time to make change. And as a result, change happens slowly in the church, and often that slowness is to the detriment of the church as the society passes it by.

While in my doctoral program, I did a study comparing literature on management in the secular world and in the church world. In my independent research, I found that until forty years ago or so, the church management literature was almost always about one hundred years behind the secular management field.[1] We have tended to resist seeing the church as an organization with a culture or as a system until recently. This has been changing even more rapidly in the past ten years or so, and that is for the better, but churches are historically slow to adopt and use the insights from the organizational development and management disciplines.

We think we are unique, and in some respects we are. But we are also human organizations. We must use the knowledge we can gain from these fields, along with other social sciences, to analyze and strengthen our organizations. Churches are unique in one way, however. We must lead our congregations with a theological eye as well.

A word about my approach: I have drawn on a wide range of experts in different fields of study, including leadership, organizational development, and theology. I also draw heavily on my own experience as a pastor, consultant, and researcher. I am a storyteller, and this book uses stories both to illustrate the points I wish to make and to help you make this material useful in your own context.

I am grateful to the many congregations and individuals who have taught me over the years and who have allowed me to work with and serve them. I have tried, as best as I can, to alter the stories I've told to protect the identities of congregations and individuals. But even with these alterations, I am telling real stories about real congregations. My prayer is that the experiences of these congregations will serve a greater purpose by aiding other congregations to become stronger and more vibrant in the mission God is calling them to in a world that so desperately needs a witness to the love, justice, and peace of God.

Is This Normal?

Accepting Change and Conflict in the Church

I was attending a pretty typical gathering of ecumenical clergy colleagues who had come together to share with and support one another—the kind of meeting that can be helpful or can devolve into complaints and whining. This particular morning we heard a little of both. One of my colleagues from a midsize congregation reported on the previous night's church council meeting. From all appearances this pastor was serving a congregation that was healthy and thriving, yet she described the council meeting as a disaster—and not atypical. The council spent its time bickering over both mundane and important things. We were all taken aback by the picture she painted of life on the inside of what seemed to be a congregation immune from conflict. What surprised me even more were her closing comments. Nearly in tears, she stated, "But these are Christians. They aren't supposed to have conflict with each other!"

Despite the popular hymn "They Will Know We Are Christians by Our Love," love, peace, and harmony are not always practiced or achieved by Christians and our churches. The vision of the church as peaceful and loving may be what we all say the church should be about, but more often than not it seems we are primed for a fight. Points of conflict range from the mundane (the color of the carpet) to the complex (human sexuality) but can also be the result of a church desperately trying to slow or even stop change.

Conflict and Change Go Hand in Hand

Conflict and change can feed into each other. Sometimes change forces conflict, and sometimes conflict forces change. Either way, where there is change, there will be conflict, and vice versa. The question is always, how do we manage both? Change is unwelcome in congregations for a variety of reasons, but they often revolve around fear of the conflict that can arise from change.

Take, for example, a congregation that was considering whether to adopt its denomination's designation for congregations that openly welcome gay, lesbian, bisexual, and transgender people. A small group met with the pastor and expressed interest in exploring this possibility. The pastor encouraged this group to talk with the leaders of the church council. The chair of the council was exceedingly nervous about bringing this matter up to the council—what was being proposed was a significant change for this congregation and destined to bring conflict—but agreed to put it on the next meeting's agenda.

One person on the council, when he realized the topic was on the agenda, began to rally others in the congregation he knew would oppose such a move. When the night of the council meeting came, this individual came prepared to announce that a "large" group of people opposed it, including a couple of big donors who had stated they would withdraw their financial support if the topic was even discussed. This person never revealed the actual number or names of the people opposed to the discussion or the names of the donors threatening to stop their giving. The council accepted the vague "large" and "a couple of," and the vagueness had its intended effect. Despite the reality that only two or three individuals opposed the discussion, it was immediately shut down out of fear of angering too many people. The chair shrugged his shoulders and said, "We tried." The small group that wanted to explore the possibility of being a welcoming church was disappointed

> Denial frequently makes appearances in congregations because such a pretense feels easier than the hard work of discernment or the harder work of changing our minds.

and angry. The pastor was frustrated. And despite the attempt to avoid conflict by shelving the discussion, division began to slowly develop in the congregation. People were angry and resentful, and those feelings went underground, only to surface later stronger and in more damaging ways.

It is human nature to resist change. Changes to what we have always known or thought or believed are difficult. Denial frequently makes appearances in some congregations. In the case of this congregation, some people wanted to deny that society and the wider church had changed on the issue of human sexuality. Such a pretense was easier than the hard work of discernment or the harder work of changing their minds.

Besides the fear of inciting conflict, leaders have other fears around change. Sometimes the opponents of change, as a way of halting change, induce fear. Other times people fear losing a stake in the system or their power in the organization. One congregation, which was already welcoming to people of diverse sexual orientations and gender identities, took up the question of marriage equality. The decision ultimately was that the pastors would not sign marriage licenses until they could be signed for all couples. A small number of people left the congregation, not because they were antigay but because they were offended and feared that the action somehow demeaned their marriage license. Another small number opposed the decision because they thought the congregation was saying there would be no more weddings. They feared they would miss participating in their children's weddings in the traditional way, such as a father walking his daughter down the aisle. Neither of these fears were based in reality. And because this change was actually managed quite well, these invalid reasons did not have any significant or long-term effect on the congregation as a whole.

There are ways we can manage change—and the inevitable conflict that comes with it—that shape both its trajectory and that of the congregation. Will everyone like everything about the change? No. Will some decide to leave as a result of change? Probably, but that is not always a bad thing. It is possible to weather disagreement and even departures if leaders intentionally and thoughtfully plan for and manage the change.

A Church in Two Worlds

We are *all* facing change in our churches. The postmodern and post-Christendom church has been called a church in transition, caught in the movement from modern to postmodern.

An apt example of thinking shaped by the modern period is the single-story television series. Each episode is built around one story, and it is told in a linear fashion from beginning to end. Usually a father or some other authority figure helps the other characters figure things out, and the dilemma presented always has a right answer. Think *Father Knows Best* or *Leave It to Beaver*. Many congregations in mainline denominations were formed in this single-story-line world. We see history as one grand narrative and believe we need to find our place in that overarching universal story. We are children of the Enlightenment and all its assumptions about reason, order, and the possibility of discovering the foundations of everything. We tend to subscribe to the notion that we can find a reason behind any phenomenon if we look hard enough and that we can appeal to an authority, such as the Bible or science, to answer our questions.

We also live with one foot in the postmodern world. This world is more like the television series *M.A.S.H.*, with multiple story lines and no one authority to solve every problem. Hawkeye Pierce, a lead character, sometimes functions as the problem solver, but he is never the sole authority to offer solutions and wisdom. In fact, Pierce is often portrayed as fallible and the "authority" in various episodes falls to others, even occasionally to characters seen as fools, such as Frank or Klinger. For the church, this postmodern world is very different from the modern. People are suspicious about the possibility of finding one definitive answer for everything and focus more on authority rooted in our experience and our stories. We still want narratives in a postmodern world but are comfortable with multiple stories based on experience. We are apprehensive of authority in any form. We don't know how to straddle the fence between the modern and the postmodern.

We also live in a post-Christendom era. In the modern period, particularly in the United States, mainline Protestantism dominated the North American cultural landscape until the mid-twentieth century. We were synonymous with society's power and authority structure. That the culture bowed to the wishes of the church was evidenced, in part, by the lack of competing activities on Sundays and, in some places, Wednesday evenings. No one wanted to give people a reason not to be at church activities—to have to choose, for example, between church and Little League or school activities.

Church is no longer people's primary focus or activity on Sunday. It is but one of myriad possibilities. The culture does not privilege Sunday morning as "church time" and therefore sacred. We have lost our position of privilege, and we don't know how to compete with all the other voices and activities. Churches have also lost members as people no longer privilege church in their lives. We may still say we belong to this church or that church, but we may not attend regularly or participate in any meaningful way. And we are at times angry at this state of affairs. We don't like our children having to choose between church and school, or church and sports, or church and really anything. This is the post-Christendom reality, however. We are not the only game in town.

The realities of losing our dominant position and of having to compete with other activities, coupled with the dwindling and aging populations in mainline Protestant churches, are frustrating at best and anger-provoking for many. These changes fuel our conflicts over more trivial matters and create a vicious circle. We want more members and yet we chase them away with our attitudes of enmity and despair.

I remember a young couple who joined a church I was pastoring saying to me that they chose our church because we were the first congregation to welcome them and not look at them as if they were a baby factory that would solve a congregation's desire for young families with children. The more we talked about what they had discovered when looking for a church, the more aware I became that they had found desperate congregations whose members thought they were being friendly but in fact made clear, "We are dying and we need young couples who are going to bring children to this place and help it grow." No one was interested in this couple as people; members saw them as the saviors in their desperation.

These postmodern and post-Christendom changes are not affecting only mainline Protestants. Roman Catholics are also struggling with these shifts, as are evangelical churches. In addition to widely discussed sexual misconduct scandals, Roman Catholic parishes are beset by conflict over the roles of women in the church (including ordination) and a structure and polity that do not adapt quickly to the realities of our contemporary world. Evangelicals appeared to be immune to the realities other Christian congregations have been facing, but studies are slowly showing they aren't. While many evangelical congregations are large enough to hide the effects of the changing culture, nevertheless their membership numbers are in decline, and they too must compete with a culture no longer interested in giving them privilege. Our culture is simply less churched, and that affects us all.

We are living in post-Christendom but long for Christendom. We are grieving the loss of what was, and in our grief we miss the opportunities that are currently before us.[1] The culture has left many congregations in the dust—many don't even recognize the changes; they just know something is different—and we have not adapted to meet that changed reality.

A good example of the church's reluctance to adapt is the physical location of many congregations. Town after small town used to be the hub of the local farming community and maybe a small industry. Most denominations built congregations in the small towns and in the cities, to serve the population majorities there. As the population moved out to the suburbs, mainline denominations didn't shift with the change, leaving many downtown churches in decline.

> We are living in post-Christendom but long for Christendom. We are grieving the loss of what was, and in our grief we miss the opportunities that are currently before us.

To further complicate the problem, many congregations have become more insular at the same time as we shrink in size and resources. We now have large and aging buildings that demand big budgets to keep them functioning. Many congregations are caught in a vicious cycle of limited resources, limited vision, and limited understanding of mission—which leads to increasingly limited resources, and around the circle again. We also lack the capacity to reach out or to welcome newcomers. Add to this situation a surrounding culture where people are generally not coming to the church, although they are interested in nurturing their spiritual lives. We fail to recognize that the church has to meet people where they are, just as Jesus did in his ministry, and consequently we do not equip ourselves to reach out or we are unwilling to minister in ways that are beyond our traditions.

Misremembering the Early Church's Perfection

I contend the church has lost its memory of who we are and who we are called to be. This is both a cause of conflict in congregations as well as a barrier to understanding conflict. We often think, like my colleague in the opening story, that conflict should not exist in a Christian community of faith. This view is rooted in a misinterpretation or even a misappropriation of the story of the early church. The idyllic vision of the early church in Acts 2:43–47 has provided a standard that Christian communities throughout the centuries have tried to live up to.

> Awe came upon everyone, because many wonders and signs were being done by the apostles. All who believed were together and had all things in common; they would sell their possessions and goods and distribute the proceeds to all, as any had need. Day by day, as they spent much time together in the temple, they broke bread at home and ate their food with glad and generous hearts, praising God and having the goodwill of all the people. And day by day the Lord added to their number those who were being saved. (Acts 2:43–47)

This utopian picture was later reinforced in Acts 4:32–35:

> Now the whole group of those who believed were of one heart and soul, and no one claimed private ownership of any possessions, but everything they owned was held in common. With great power the apostles gave their testimony to the resurrection of the Lord Jesus, and great grace was upon them all. There was not a needy person among them, for as many as owned lands or houses sold them and brought the proceeds of what was sold. They laid it at the apostles' feet, and it was distributed to each as any had need.

These visions have haunted congregations and led us to think that the early believers were perfect in their devotion to the apostles' teaching, to fellowship, to worship and prayer. We interpret these passages, "They were one big happy family."

We forget that the early church's perfection begins to unravel in Acts 5 and 6. Acts 5 introduces treachery within the church with the deception of Ananias and Sapphira. Acts 6 continues to reveal the conflicted nature of the early church with the complaints of the Hellenists against the Hebrew Christians over prejudice against the Greek widows. Paul and Peter argue over the outreach to the Gentiles at the Jerusalem Council. In addition to the accounts of conflict and dispute recorded in Acts, we find that Paul addresses varied conflicts in his letters. The unfolding picture of the early church is anything but idyllic.

> We are often uncertain as to whether we should tolerate bad behavior because we are the church and we are supposed to help people. Yet drawing clear boundaries around bad behavior may be the best way to help people who are struggling.

The disputes and deceptions we encounter in the Acts of the Apostles don't sound all that different from the issues involved in congregations today. The question of who belongs and who doesn't is still prevalent. We no longer argue about whether folks need to be Jewish before they can be Christians, but we debate whether we'll welcome gay, lesbian, bisexual, and transgender people. We still struggle with racism. We struggle with class distinctions. As Ecclesiastes 1:9 reminds us, "There is nothing new under the sun." We share much in common with the early church when it comes to conflict.

Conflict and Change: What Do We Really Mean?

Before we proceed any further, we need to be clear what we mean by *conflict* and *change*. We'll go into greater detail in later chapters, but for now, conflict is any situation where there is more than one opinion about an issue or subject. It is not a fight, although it may result in fights. It is simply the existence of more than one opinion, and conflict resolution is how those differences are worked out and how the congregation moves forward.

Conflict is most often specific and focuses on particular issues. Conflict is always present in our lives, but it waxes and wanes in raising our anxiety levels.

Change is always present because it is a reflection of the continual movement, growth, and decline of individuals, organizations, and cultures. We age. Organizations age. The way we see things, react, and live at different stages of our lives changes. The culture around us changes, and we are forced to respond to it, whether we like it or not.

Without change, we die. If our bodies do not grow from infancy to adulthood, there is something wrong, causing serious illness, if not death. Our relationships, such as marriage, carry a trajectory of continued understanding of each other, encouraging each person to grow and accomplish things, or the relationship stagnates and dies. Organizations must continue to develop beyond their formation or they never reach a level of sustainability. Change is necessary for healthy and productive living.

Is Conflict Simply Bad Behavior?

A pastor friend of mine once told a neighboring congregation she was consulting with that they had too high a tolerance for bad behavior. Members had been fighting, and a few congregants were trying to bully others into agreeing with them on a number of issues. Tolerance for people acting out and bullying is evident in many congregations. The primary reason folks in churches think conflict is bad is that we immediately associate it with bad behavior—ugliness, name-calling, lying, and a host of other unsavory and un-Christian behaviors. We need to learn to separate the conflict from the behaviors, so we are able to see more clearly the real issues at hand. We cannot avoid conflict, but we can avoid bad behavior.

Churches attract people with many different physical, mental, emotional, and spiritual problems. Even Jesus said that those who are well are in no need of a doctor, but that he had come to heal the sick (Matthew 9:12). People in need contribute to conflict out of our own neediness. Sometimes this neediness is rooted in issues like mental illness, family dysfunction, or addiction, and it manifests in bad behavior at church. Church leaders and congregants are often uncertain as to whether we should tolerate bad behavior in such instances, because we are the church and we are supposed to help people. Yet drawing clear boundaries around bad behavior may be the best way to help people who are struggling.

I am reminded of a congregation I worked with that had a woman in her late fifties who faithfully came to church every Sunday and volunteered on various committees and groups and in the church office. She was mentally ill, with the illness presenting itself sometimes in subtle ways and other times in ways that were destructive to the people around her. She was one of those folks who could suck the air out of a room just by entering it.

> A tremendous amount of damage has been done in congregations by leaders ignoring conflict under the misguided assumption that to address the conflict would hurt people's feelings, stir up more trouble, or compromise their jobs. When conflict arises, people are already hurting, and failing to address the issue only leads to more pain.

Her behavior in small groups or committees led people to avoid activities they knew she would attend. People resigned in droves from committees she joined. She particularly wanted to "welcome" new members or visitors and would do so by telling them how awful things were at the church or how incompetent the pastor was. None of what she shared was true, but it discouraged new members and visitors alike from getting involved and bonding with the congregation. As a volunteer in the office, she had access to the mail and the voicemail system. She would read private mail that had been left in staff members' church mailboxes. She often accessed the voicemail of various staff and listened to what were theoretically confidential messages. Then in meetings she shared this information out of context and without any regard for the sensitive nature of her revelations.

Yet no one would take her on, for fear that she would find ways to attack and undermine their standing in the church. The leaders also held the misconception that one cannot fire volunteers or church members. A few people attempted over the years to rein her in. Leaders met with her and told her the bad behavior had to stop, and it would abate somewhat, for a little while, but she would soon be back to her old ways. She was told at one point that she could come to worship but was not allowed to participate in any activities outside of Sunday worship. She would come to worship and continue to sow seeds of discontent as she talked with people after the service.

Finally, the church elected a new head of the church council, who decided enough was enough. The new leader got the backing of the council and the staff, then met with the woman and told her that she was no longer allowed to come to the church or participate in any activities. The leader laid out various documented incidents of the problem behavior and told her that the congregation could not tolerate such behavior anymore. The collective sigh of relief in the congregation was amazing, and things soon began to normalize in the committees and groups she had been a part of. Boundaries had been drawn in order to quash the bad behavior, and now the congregation as a whole could move forward.

The Role of Leaders in Conflict

Leaders, both pastoral and lay, can be a source of conflict or a salve for it. As evidenced in the story above, conflict is caused or heightened when leaders fail to address the source of trouble—whether it is caused by human failure or bad behavior or both—in a manner that is theologically grounded and seeks healing for the community.

At times leaders simply want to avoid conflict rather than deal constructively with it. Passivity can have harmful consequences, however. One pastor I worked with would routinely tell everyone who came to him with an idea that it was great and that they should pursue it. He never wanted to disappoint anyone or take a stand on an idea. Unfortunately no one was coordinating the ideas put forward, and some of them conflicted with each other. In addition, he didn't ask if the idea fit within the mission of the church or if it was part of God's calling for the congregation. Consequently council meetings often devolved into angry shouting matches, with one person proclaiming that the pastor had said her idea was good and another person saying the pastor had told him his (opposing) idea was good. The pastor refused to own the confusion he had created. The church remained in turmoil until a strong and wise lay leader helped develop a process for vetting new ideas, a system that included the pastor but did not rely solely on him.

A tremendous amount of damage has been done in congregations by leaders ignoring conflict under the misguided assumption that to address the conflict would hurt people's feelings, stir up more trouble, or compromise their jobs. I don't want to minimize the fact that some clergy have lost their jobs when they stood up to conflict. But often the fear of losing our jobs holds us back, even though we may not lose our jobs in reality.

We need to be clear with ourselves when we address conflict that when it arises, people are already hurting, and failing to address the issue only leads to more pain. True, conflict resolution may not be painless, but better to endure pain that is part of a healing process than allow the wounds of unresolved conflict to fester.

> What a powerful witness to a troubled and conflicted world when a congregation is able to work through conflict and emerge stronger in our vision and commitment to the reign of God on earth.

When addressing bad behavior and conflict, leaders need to find a balance between the individual's needs and the needs of the congregation. This is best achieved by taking time to fully understand the problems contributing to the conflict. For instance, a church choir I once directed had a member who could not carry a tune. He was always off-key, and he sang loudly. Choir members complained about his singing and asked me to ask him to leave the choir. What the choir members did not know was that this man had recently gone through a painful divorce, and his foray into the church and the choir in particular were important to him because they helped meet his need for community and healing. I struck a compromise with the choir. I would ask Bert to sing more quietly and would signal him if he got too loud, and they would welcome him in their midst. The compromise worked for all concerned, and the conflict that had been growing dissipated quickly.

The Upside of Conflict and Change

Conflict and change themselves are not unhealthy or evil. Though they may manifest in behaviors that are unhealthy or evil, conflict and change are actually neutral, natural, and normal and can serve many useful purposes in congregations. In the throes of conflict and change, people are able to articulate concerns and come together to heal brokenness and pain. Working together through conflict will help us discover synergetic solutions to problems facing the church and the world. We have an opportunity to be stronger witnesses and grow as Christians through the process of resolving conflict. The question is, are congregational members and leaders committed to resolving conflict in a healthy and theologically grounded manner? Are we willing to do the hard work necessary to live as Christians known not for our conflict, disagreements, or self-interest but for our love through difficulty?

I am not suggesting that Christians should always agree. We will not. What turns legitimate disagreement in the church to evil and destruction are the reactions and actions of people who put self-interest or the pursuit of power above the welfare of the community. Disastrous results occur when we cease to work at discerning God's will for the situation and our future and put personal issues before the community's issues. In a more positive vein, what a powerful witness to a troubled and conflicted world when a congregation is able to work through conflict and emerge stronger in our vision and commitment to the reign of God on earth.

Reflecting on Your Congregation . . .

1. How is conflict understood in your congregation?

   Is change welcomed or resisted?

2. What is your congregation's history of dealing with significant changes?

   What is your congregation's history of addressing conflict?

3. Describe some major conflicts you have had to work through. What happened, and how was it resolved (if it was)?

   If it was not resolved, what happened and how have you addressed it since?

   What was leaders' role in the resolution?

What Are We So Afraid Of?

Using Scripture, History, and Theology to Reframe Our Perspective

You could have heard a pin drop in the room when I unveiled the definition of "church" that came to light in my work with this typical mainline congregation. It could have been a church anywhere in the United States and in any mainline denomination. Plagued by years of conflict and bullying behavior by a few members, this midsize congregation had just lost its pastor—again. With one exception, a pastor had left the congregation or been fired about every seven years. If there is such a thing as a seven-year itch, this congregation had it repeatedly. I was engaged to help them figure out what was going on and how they might find new and better ways of being a community of faith.

With the help of a small team of volunteers, I interviewed sixty members of the congregation, ranging from the most involved to those on the margins. We asked questions about significant spiritual moments, favorite memories, how the church dealt with conflict, and other issues. Analysis of the interview summaries revealed several perspectives functioning within the congregation. Key among them was the congregation's definition of church. I met with the small group assigned to oversee this re-envisioning and conflict-resolution process and revealed my findings from the interview data.

I wrote the following equation on a white board:

Happy + Nice = Church

I then sat down and waited for their response. Dumbfounded, they all stared at the equation for a relatively long time, and then someone said, "Shouldn't God be somewhere in the equation?" "Exactly," I responded. "I would have been happy with God or Jesus or even the Holy Spirit, but no one mentioned them." In the survey, none of the congregants interviewed mentioned church-related experiences in response to the question about significant spiritual moments. No one talked about God in the answer to any question. The key things they wanted from a pastor were that she make them happy and keep the peace. The result was stunning and pointed to several key strategies to address the apparent absence of God from congregational life. Dealing with that concern was foundational to solving the congregation's systemic issues long term, learning how to communicate, and eliminating the acceptance of bullying behavior.

> By rethinking what it means to be a church—using Scripture, history, and the Holy Spirit as keystones—we can reconnect with our sacred mission and address conflict and change in more positive ways.

The inability to understand God as the source of the congregation's life and calling severely damaged this congregation's ability to fully be the church—to be a place for members' and others' faith formation and a springboard for mission. Focusing only internally and seeing the members themselves as the source and goal of their community had prevented them from effectively addressing conflict when it arose. This internal focus also kept them from knowing what they wanted and needed in a pastoral leader and developing any sense of mission to guide them through change. Without God in the equation, this congregation struggled to find a sense of purpose beyond being simply a social club.

Rethinking Our Approach to Conflict and Change

In some ways, this congregation's understanding of the church is not atypical. Many congregations are internally focused, operating with the perspective that church is about being nice to one another, that conflict should not exist, and that the call of the Christian life is to be happy. We overlook our original vision and purpose: to be followers of Jesus Christ, coming together to worship God and discern God's call to our assembly and to us as individuals. Churches forget that our calling is to serve people in need. And we forget that this work is fraught with the challenges of finding collective agreement as individuals interpret faith and mission, and work together to discern the best use of shared—and often limited—resources.

The church is a place where the private worlds of individual faith intersect with the public world in unique and important ways. While the theories and processes that guide secular organizations are applicable—and beneficial—to the church, they are not enough. As we will explore, the role the social sciences and organizational development play in church leadership is important, but because of the God dimension, churches need something more theological than just secular theory. Part of our struggle in addressing conflict in the church is that many conflict resolution methods make more use of social sciences than of our deep theological convictions and resources. We need both, however, to understand our inner workings and vision for mission. God must be in the equation.

Recognizing that our vision for mission comes from God also helps us reframe what conflict is about. To participate in the *missio Dei*, the mission of God, the church will experience conflict and change. It comes with the territory. We fulfill this mission—sharing the Gospel—primarily by practicing reconciliation, transformation, hospitality, and love. We are called to bring the realm of God to the wider community, and that realm is not always a comfortable place. We are called to leave our comfort zones and work for justice, right relationship, and people in need. Agreeing on who these people are and how best to serve them can be difficult. Without a theological grounding for working with conflict and change, we are simply trying to manage the anxiety and behavior that surround these issues.

> Churches forget that our calling is to serve people in need. And we forget that this work is fraught with the challenges of finding collective agreement as individuals interpret faith and mission, and work together to discern the best use of shared—and often limited—resources.

Several resources are available to aid us in rethinking conflict and change in the church. First, we can draw on the witness of Scripture and the story it tells about the history of conflict and change for people of faith in ancient Israel and the early church. We see that conflict and change are a given in being church. Second, we can explore the witness of the church's tradition and history, which is filled with conflict and constant change. And third, we can turn to the rich theologies regarding the Holy Spirit and the role of the Spirit in the life of the church. Together, these three resources give us as churches a different way to approach transition in a culture that no longer privileges religion, resulting in massive change and conflict for congregations. And as we'll see, they can help us keep God in the center of our actions and our community.

Reframing Our Perspective: Scripture

When conflict or change arises, most leaders and members of churches are interested in either tamping it down, minimizing it, or making it go away. We tend to have a strong desire to return to status quo. The uncomfortable feelings, the anxiety, and the fear or reality of bad behavior many exhibit in the midst of conflict and change send us all running for the fastest fix we can find to make the unpleasantness go away. And yet it doesn't go away. Change will happen whether we want it to or not. Conflict may go underground, but it will return to haunt us in ways sometimes more damaging than if we had just dealt with it in the first place.

The Free Community

As we learned in chapter 1, the early church was rife with conflict, most notably detailed in the Acts of the Apostles. We can learn a great deal from the way Paul deals with the early church in his Epistles. There we find examples of resolving conflict rather than trying to ignore it. When Paul writes to churches experiencing conflict and seeking advice, his counsel is sometimes pastoral but can also be challenging, such as in the first letter to the Corinthians. The familiar passages in 1 Corinthians 12 and 13 are prime examples of Paul's pastoral nature. He challenges the church at Corinth by reminding them that God has given many gifts and calls them into many activities, but they are still one body in Christ, without distinctions dividing them. While it may be human nature to put some ahead of others because of their status or heritage or gifts, it is not God's way. God binds all together in love and that is the greatest gift of all.

Paul offers the Corinthians a metaphor to help them understand their divisions as being gifts from God, not sources of conflict. The gifts are given for the building up of the body. Paul continues with the famous "love chapter," telling them, "If I have prophetic powers, and understand all mysteries and all knowledge, and if I have all faith, so as to remove mountains, but do not have love, I am nothing" (1 Corinthians 13:2).

Paul's challenge to the Corinthian church is often taken as instruction for individuals and is a favorite at weddings. But we need to remember it was written to a congregation. It is about love in community.

Other times Paul is direct and even angry, as he is in the letter to the Galatians. (See especially Galatians 3:1–5.) Members of the Galatian church are struggling with false teachers who are leading them astray, in Paul's estimation. He is furious that these teachers are confusing the Galatians and frustrated with the church for letting them spread their nonsense. Paul's language seems even harsh as he chastises the Galatians for letting others mislead them as opposed to relying on the Holy Spirit. Paul minces no words here. His is not the sort of language we would use today, but we can see how far Paul will go to make his point. He wasn't aiming merely to make people happy and keep the peace, as we so often do today.

> While it may be human nature to put some ahead of others because of their status or heritage or gifts, it is not God's way. God binds all together in love and that is the greatest gift of all.

In fact, Paul encourages debate when he uses the Greek city-state, or polis, as a metaphor for the church in Philippians 1, the introduction to the passage often called the Christ hymn. According to New Testament professor David Fredrickson in his commentary on Philippians, Paul is using the polis as a way to emphasize that the freedom Christ has given members of the church is the freedom to come together and debate the future of the church, just the way free Greek citizens came together to debate the future of the city.[1]

Fredrickson comes to this conclusion from his examination of Philippians 1:27, where Paul states:

Only, live your life in a manner worthy of the gospel of Christ, so that, whether I come and see you or am absent and hear about you, I will know that you are standing firm in one spirit, striving side by side with one mind for the faith of the gospel.

The argument Fredrickson makes is that Paul is using the Greek word *polisthuesthe* in his phrase "live your life in a manner." *Polisthuesthe* refers to how the community is to engage in political debate. The Christian community is to live in a manner similar to the political world of the Greek city-state, where citizens debate one another. The metaphor Paul uses here and in other places in his letters is one we rarely call upon for understanding the church, but it is an invitation to engage, debate, and, in essence, enter into change and potential conflict as a church. As Paul shows us, this call to engage with one another is Christ's gift of freedom to us.

> Paul invites us to engage, debate, and, in essence, enter into change and potential conflict as a church. This call to engage with one another is Christ's gift of freedom to us.

The Reconciling Community

Reconciliation is not about everyone thinking the same or about everyone being in total agreement. Such a goal is unrealistic and disrespects the diversity of experience, thought, and opinion present in the church community. Reconciliation is a much more complex process. Reconciliation seeks to honor diversity while guiding the way to discerning God's desire for the congregation as a whole. While many passages in Scripture expound on reconciliation and describe the church as a reconciling community, this passage identifies reconciliation—achieving an all-inclusive, open, and welcoming community that respects diversity and seeks to heal animosity among people—as one of the church's primary missions.

A helpful example from Paul's letters comes from 2 Corinthians 5:16–21, which sheds light on the ministry of reconciliation the church is called to participate in as faithful followers of Jesus Christ:

From now on, therefore, we regard no one from a human point of view; even though we once knew Christ from a human point of view, we know him no longer in that way. So if anyone is in Christ, there is a new creation: everything old has passed away; see, everything has become new! All this is from God, who reconciled us to himself through Christ, and has given us the ministry of reconciliation; that is, in Christ God was reconciling the world to himself, not counting their trespasses against them, and entrusting the message of reconciliation to us. So we are ambassadors for Christ, since God is making his appeal through us; we entreat you on behalf of Christ, be reconciled to God. For our sake he made him to be sin who knew no sin, so that in him we might become the righteousness of God. (2 Corinthians 5:16–21)

These few verses offer a basis for our thinking about the church as a reconciling community. The conflict in the Corinthian church arises from an old way of seeing. Paul argues that Christians are to see differently as the new creation in Christ, not from a human point of view, but from God's point of view—seeing things as they really are and not through the deceiving lens of human perception. This view is the result of God restoring us to God's self in Christ.

> Reconciliation is not about everyone thinking the same or about everyone being in total agreement. Reconciliation seeks to honor diversity while guiding the way to discerning God's desire for the congregation as a whole.

In 2005 the United Church of Christ's General Synod took up a resolution in support of marriage equality for all people. It was highly controversial, and many of the delegates to the synod had been instructed by their home congregations to vote against the resolution. These instructions violated the usual protocol for delegates, who are supposed to come to synod open to the leading of the Holy Spirit through the discussion and debate and then determine how they are being led to vote on a measure before the synod. Due to the tension around the resolution, the planners of the General Synod held a series of conversations for delegates that involved Scripture study, prayer, and deep listening to one another about marriage. Everyone was encouraged to share in an open, honest, and calm way their own thoughts on what marriage is and what encouraging marriage for lesbian and gay people would mean for their understanding of marriage as a church. The conversations were powerful, and people on opposite sides of the issue found themselves able to share with one another in a respectful way.

Likewise, when the resolution came to the floor of the synod, the debate was impassioned but respectful. Delegates were asked to refrain from applauding or making any verbal responses to speakers. Prayer was called for several times during the debate and before the vote. After the vote, prayer was again offered to bring the assembly together. The resolution passed, with a great number of delegates reporting that they had come prepared to vote against the resolution and yet after entering the process in a spirit of discernment, felt led to change their votes. The decision to change their minds was painful for some of the delegates, knowing they would go home to face anger and dismay over their decision, but it was how they felt God was leading them to vote.

The aftermath of the vote was quite mixed and often painful. Some congregations left the denomination and others joined. But those who participated in that General Synod, no matter their individual vote, had a deep and rich sense of being one as a church in the discernment and decision making. Delegates did not all agree, but there was also no animosity. People felt they had been heard and respected. Those who voted against the resolution felt pain, and those who voted for it were joyful, but people did not focus on those emotions. They left the floor of synod quietly and reverently. Rather than focusing on who won and who lost, the moment was viewed as sacred and historic.

The Community of Transformation

The new way of seeing that Paul talks about in 2 Corinthians 5 calls the church to a new way of being and doing as well. On the cross Jesus did something new. He conquered death by submitting to it. God blessed that submission and raised Christ from the dead. Death and sin could no longer bind those who live in the way of the cross and the empty tomb. In *Paul for Everyone: 2 Corinthians*, leading Bible scholar N. T. Wright says, "Paul is saying that in Christ, something new *has* happened and therefore something new *must now* happen."[2] The church has a significant role to play in carrying out the call for something new to happen. This ministry of reconciliation to which the church is called is about transformation. We are called into a new way, and our lives as individuals and as faith communities are transformed. This call extends to every aspect of the church—denominations, midlevel judicatories, and congregations. God calls the church to live into the death and resurrection of Jesus by following in his way. The way of Christ is one of reconciling all to God. The transformation that results is demanding and countercultural. The church can no longer go about our business as usual. We cannot be just like any other human institution. The church must live differently—as transformed and reconciled people. This is the good news we have to share with the world—respect for diversity, harmony among differences, and peace with one another.

> The church must live differently—as transformed and reconciled people. This is the good news we have to share with the world—respect for diversity, harmony among differences, and peace with one another.

Transformation can take many forms. It can be about relationships within the church, and it can also be about how the church relates to the world around us. Serving in ministry in the upper Midwest, I have often observed congregations founded by groups that immigrated to the region well over a century ago still trying to retain their cultural roots. This is all well and good until the loyalty to those roots begins to die off with its aging membership, yet the few members who cling to that affiliation can stifle the ability of the church to respond to a new generation.

Lutheran churches where the hymn boards and other church decorations are still in Norwegian or Swedish look more like museums than living, breathing congregations responding to the needs of people in the twenty-first century. Former German Evangelical and Reformed congregations in the United Church of Christ where individuals still talk fondly of the good old days when the service was in German can alienate younger generations who cannot fathom why we would speak anything other than

English in worship. And, of course, the plea in some of those churches to return to the Heidelberg Catechism as the primary resource for faith formation is even more baffling to younger generations, who see catechisms as restrictive, dogmatic, and unrelated to their own lives.

To be a community of transformation means being countercultural but not a historic anomaly. Learning to be countercultural by loving our differences, respecting all, and learning to work together in peace for a common mission defies the culture around us. But we are also called to speak to that culture. Too often we seem to be from another century in our choice of music, our way of worshipping, and the aesthetics of the sanctuary and the rest of the church building. While it is important to affirm our connection to the church throughout the ages, sometimes we can appear to the outside world to speak as a relic from the past. We are called to be living witnesses to the power of God's love in our midst, not museums preserving the past. We either answer this call or we continue to be increasingly out of touch with the world around us—and to decline.

> To be a community of transformation means being countercultural but not a historic anomaly.

The Community of Ambassadors

Paul's argument that the church is called to reconciliation and transformation, based on the work of Christ, calls us to continue Christ's work by joining with God in Christ's life and mission. Christians do not replace Christ, but rather serve as ambassadors for Christ. An ambassador speaks in the name of the one she represents. Ambassadors seek to promote well-being, peace, and communication between two potential enemies. With even a cursory knowledge of diplomatic work, we must acknowledge that this is difficult and sometimes delicate work. The further apart the parties' points of view, the more work is required to bring them to agreement, at least on common values and goals. While God is with us in this work, we have to learn to listen, share honestly, address differences, respect the other, and work in good faith. Staying with the conversation takes time and commitment. Finding a way through when we appear to be facing an impasse takes creativity and imagination. We model our efforts on the work God did in Christ. God, the reconciler, came in Jesus to join the world to God's self and has entrusted the church—us—with the task of continuing that work as ambassadors for Christ. This restoration of human-divine union is at the heart of the church's mission. We are ambassadors beyond ourselves, not for ourselves.

We can find countless examples of people who have gone out from churches to support others in conflicted and even dangerous places and events. People have taken such actions around the globe—in the Middle East, in South Africa before apartheid was ended, in Central America, and most recently in Ferguson, Missouri, where a white police officer fatally shot an unarmed black teen. The incident sparked widespread protests and violent civil unrest. As I write, several colleagues of mine are in the St. Louis area organizing groups to witness interactions in Ferguson between the police and the townspeople in the aftermath of the shooting. Some of these groups are present just to try to maintain peace and stop further violence. Others are working to bring the various parties together to try to find a more permanent and just solution to the racism and resultant violence present in the town. They are not seeking to convert, but to be ambassadors for a different way for people to live together. Their mission is born out of their faith and commitment to live differently, to live in the way Christ called them to live. Their witness is powerful.

> Restoration of human-divine union is at the heart of the church's mission. We are ambassadors beyond ourselves, not for ourselves.

The Balanced Community: God, Neighbor, Self

Other examples of Jesus's teachings that help us restore God to the center of our community and rethink conflict and change in the church are those of the commandments, specifically the Great Commandment, found in Matthew, Mark, and Luke. Each Gospel places Jesus in a slightly different setting, but in all three, he names the first two commandments in response to someone asking, What is the greatest commandment? Jesus is being tested to see whether he really is faithful to his Jewish tradition and a legitimate teacher and rabbi. Jesus passes the test and then he exceeds the questioners' expectations, as we see here in Matthew:

When the Pharisees heard that he had silenced the Sadducees, they gathered together, and one of them, a lawyer, asked him a question to test him. "Teacher, which commandment in the law is the greatest?" He said to him, "You shall love the Lord your God with all your heart, and with all your soul, and with all your mind. This is the greatest and first commandment. And a second is like it: You shall love your neighbor as yourself. On these two commandments hang all the law and the prophets." (Matthew 22:34–40)

Jesus responds with the *Shema*, a central tenet of Jewish life and liturgy from Deuteronomy 6:5 that instructs Israel to put God first, above all else—which Jesus does. But then he adds to the first commandment a second one that ties loving our neighbor to the first commandment and loving our neighbor to loving one's own self. These two commandments in Jesus's ethic are the pinnacle of the entire law and the prophets. All comes to rest on loving God completely and loving our neighbor and loving ourselves. This ethic makes for a complete relationship between God, the neighbor, and the self.

> The commitment to loving God, self, and neighbor gives us a sharper focus for relationships within a congregation, forming the heart of congregational life and a congregation's ability to ride the waves of change and conflict.

Likewise in congregations, we are called to love God first and then to love each other as we love ourselves, creating balance in our relationships. We are not to disregard personal needs, but they are in balance with loving relationship with others within and outside the congregation. We do not love ourselves at the expense of each other. The commitment to loving God, self, and neighbor gives us a sharper focus for relationships within a congregation, forming the heart of congregational life and a congregation's ability to ride the waves of change and conflict.

The Hebrew Scriptures also offer us other principles that affect our perspective on conflict and change, focusing on relationships. The ancient tradition of hospitality is crucial to Israel's life as a community. When

Israel falls out of favor with God, the problem is usually that Israel has violated the hospitality ethic in some way. The hospitality ethic is basic for everything Israel must do, including welcoming the stranger, widows, orphans, travelers—essentially anyone and everyone. This ethic is woven early on into the fabric of Israel's understanding of the Law and God's covenant with Israel.

> You shall not wrong or oppress a resident alien, for you were aliens in the land of Egypt. You shall not abuse any widow or orphan. If you do abuse them, when they cry out to me, I will surely heed their cry; my wrath will burn, and I will kill you with the sword, and your wives shall become widows and your children orphans. (Exodus 22:21–24)

This is a moral imperative for Israel that pushes the nation not to be insular and focus only on itself, but commands the people to attend to the needs of the "other."

As we have seen above, Scripture points to our call to engage and become agents of change and reconcilers of conflict—with God always at the center of our actions and intentions. The history of the people of faith throughout Scripture is one of continual change and conflict as Israel, the disciples, and the early church seek to follow the calling of God. The process was one of trial and error. Being a witness to the God who called them into being and sent them out to serve also entailed great risk taking.

We are called to engage and become agents of change and reconcilers of conflict—with God always at the center of our actions and intentions.

Members of one church I worked with found themselves with a "good" conflict to sort out, albeit a risky one. On the north end of its lot, the church had a decent piece of property with a single-family house on it. Over many years the church had housed refugee families in it. The idea began to grow that this piece of property could be put to a larger and greater use. The project took a couple of years of dreaming, discussing, and disagreeing before members finally came to the conclusion that the property would be a wonderful location for a multifamily housing complex dedicated to "work force" housing.

Such housing is intended for people who are working but can't afford to rent market-rate apartments in the city.

The decision to do this large project was fraught with conflict internally and externally, but people felt strongly that God was calling them to undertake the project. Questions arose about who knew how to build such a place, how to fund it, what to do about parking, how to function as a landlord. The list went on and on. One by one, the task force charged with exploring the project found answers and talked more with the congregation, and the day finally came when the congregation voted nearly unanimously to proceed.

The congregation then faced a conflict they couldn't have imagined. The local neighborhood went up in arms over building housing to serve poor people. The congregation found itself the target of anger and unfair accusations. Neighbors and local businesses launched a campaign to try to stop the housing project. The congregation, however, never wavered from its commitment to building the apartment complex. Their commitment was rooted in answering a call from God, and while they didn't like being the target of misinformation and anger, they never backed down. In fact, they learned how to deal with the politics of the situation and to stand up to the threats. They also began a campaign of their own to patronize local businesses and let owners and employees know church members were their customers. Eventually the furor calmed down, the city backed the project, and relationships with the neighborhood were rebuilt. Today a beautiful, well-maintained, and well-managed multifamily dwelling sits on the property and is full of residents who otherwise would be homeless or living in less desirable situations. The project is an asset to the community, and members of the congregation believe they followed God's call. Their understanding of the call of God was deeply rooted in the scriptural witness, and they saw themselves continuing the work of their ancestors in faith. They have gone on to other daring projects to engage with the local community and now even the global community. By functioning as a balanced

> Remembering our history and the conflict that our forebears came through is a hopeful sign that we, too, can survive and even thrive in conflict.

community, they are seeking to bring God's message of love and reconciliation to the world around them.

Reframing Our Perspective: Historical Resources

The history of Christianity contains one conflict after another. Perhaps the greatest example of conflict as a natural and normal part of our history is the Reformation, the sixteenth-century religious and cultural upheaval that occurred when Reformers like Martin Luther and John Calvin questioned the Catholic Church's authority.

Non-Catholic and non-Orthodox Christians are generally referred to as Protestants, which is rooted in the Latin word for "protest," *protestari*. *Protest* originally meant "to make a solemn declaration" but became associated over time with making that declaration in opposition to a dominant point of view. Such points of view could be political or religious, and in the sixteenth century they were both. While scholars debate the exact origin of the term "Protestant," it still signifies a group or groups of people who stand against the theological views of Roman Catholicism. Therefore, the history of all Protestant churches' origin and development is one of conflict. So we should not be surprised when conflict arises in our congregations today.

Remembering our history and the conflict that our forebears came through is a hopeful sign that we, too, can survive and even thrive in conflict. More importantly, it is a reminder that God can use us and our conflicts to further God's mission for the world.

Conflict Among the Reformers

The Reformers themselves had tremendous conflicts with one another. Martin Luther was originally the focus of the conflicts with Rome, but then others began to establish other non-Catholic churches and came into direct conflict with Luther. One of the most famous of these conflicts was between Luther and Ulrich Zwingli, a Swiss Reformer who pushed even further than Luther to redefine the church and doctrine, particularly an understanding of the Eucharist or Holy Communion. Luther and Zwingli came together at a meeting that became known as the Marburg Colloquy in October 1529. While they could agree on many points of doctrine, they could not find common ground on the Eucharist.

Luther insisted on the real presence of Christ in the consecrated elements of bread and wine. He defined "real presence" differently from Roman Catholic doctrine, but nevertheless believed strongly that Christ was actually present in the elements. Zwingli insisted that the elements of bread and wine were merely symbolic representations of Christ's body and blood. The famous and perhaps apocryphal story of the colloquy is that Luther stormed out after writing on the table between the two men, "This is my body." This episode, while the one most remembered about Marburg, doesn't reflect the greater accomplishment that Luther came to the colloquy doubting whether Zwingli was actually Christian and left admitting he was Christian but that they held significant differences of opinion.

They did agree on many points, one of which was a shared lack of respect for the Anabaptist movement. The significant disagreement with the Anabaptists was over their refusal to baptize children. In sixteenth-century Germany, baptism made one not only a Christian, but a citizen. The Anabaptists were pacifists, and by refusing to baptize their children, they also refused to make their children citizens, so—as noncitizens—they couldn't be drafted into military service. This issue was about more than a sacrament; it was a political disagreement. Neither Luther nor Zwingli understood pacifism as Christian teaching, and they had no qualms about the church and the state being one system. They merely wanted a church other than the Roman Catholic Church to share power with the state.

The Donatist Controversy

Luther, Zwingli, and the Anabaptists weren't the first people after the close of the early church period to disagree with one another. The formation of doctrine and the creeds, understandings of the efficacy of ministry, and many other issues were sources of conflict after conflict in the history of the Christian church. One conflict that was crucial from the late third century into the fourth century became known as the Donatist controversy. It was such a significant conflict that it resulted in a schism in the Christian churches in northern Africa that lasted into the sixth century. The essence of the conflict was over the standing of clergy who had renounced their faith during the persecutions by the Roman emperor Diocletian and those who hadn't. Those who refused to denounce their faith were normally martyred. Those who denied the faith survived, and after the persecution ended they wanted to return to ministry. However, the Donatists claimed that these priests were no longer worthy of priestly ministry and furthermore that any sacrament or pastoral act they performed was null and void. The schism took place between those who agreed with this rigid view and those who forgave the priests and allowed them to return to ministry.

While there was no declaration on the efficacy of the ministry of these priests, the general belief in the West was that the sacraments and other rites performed by these apostate priests were still valid and that the efficacy of the sacrament didn't depend on the state of the priest's soul. This view has prevailed since the fourth century, but the question still arises during times of tension and disagreement in the church, both Roman Catholic and Protestant. The more recent tragedies around clergy sexual misconduct have again raised the question. Having worked with a great many cases of misconduct, I have been asked more than once whether a baptism or a marriage is valid if the pastor or priest who officiated had committed sexual misconduct. These controversies and conflicts plague our history as Christians, and it is helpful to examine how we did or didn't weather them as examples of ways to move beyond them.

> The formation of doctrine and the creeds, understandings of the efficacy of ministry, and many other issues were sources of conflict after conflict in the history of the Christian church.

Development of the Creeds

The development of the various articles of the creeds was also surrounded by a great deal of conflict. Without going into too much detail here, we can say Christians' basic understandings of the nature of Christ and the nature of the Trinity, particularly with respect to the Holy Spirit, unfolded through a long history of fighting, excommunications, schisms, and other less than exemplary behavior on the part of our ancestors. The split between the Western church and the Orthodox churches over the "filioque clause" and the origin of the Holy Spirit continues to this day. *Filioque* is a Latin phrase meaning "and the Son." Simply put, the First Council of Constantinople in 381 stated, "We believe in the Holy Spirit, the Lord, the giver of life, who proceeds from the Father, who with the

Father and the Son is worshipped and glorified." Two centuries later, the Synod of Toledo in 589 added the phrase known as the filioque clause, so that the creed would read, "We believe in the Holy Spirit, the Lord, the giver of life, who proceeds from the Father *and the Son*" (emphasis mine). This addition would become a constant source of disagreement between churches in the East and West until the churches in the East split from Rome in 1054. Known as the Great Schism, this split gave Christianity what would become known as the Orthodox churches. The split has never healed, although there is now less animosity and more cooperation between the churches than there was for many centuries.

Contemporary Conflicts

The history of the church is also filled with incredible examples of the church as healer, reconciler, and witness to a different way of life. Both small Christian communities and larger movements have been present to transform situations where there is conflict. Most of us view Christian history with a focus on the larger institutional structures, and we forget the prolific activity behind that picture. Historian and author Diana Butler Bass refers to this forgetting as "spiritual amnesia."[3] We simply don't know or remember many of the stories present in our own history, even our local histories.

> Most of us view Christian history with a focus on the larger institutional structures, and we forget the prolific activity behind that picture. We simply don't know or remember many of the stories present in our own history, even our local histories.

The congregation where I was ordained was in the midst of a great deal of conflict during the period when I was active there. The church was long past its glory days. It was divided between a group of stalwarts who had been members for a long time, as had their families before them, and a group of newcomers who reflected the community now surrounding the church. The newcomers had a vision for a church that would play a vital role in the city it now served, and the stalwarts wanted to continue to hold up a vision of the historic, white, and upper-middle-class, even wealthy, church of the past. The newcomers didn't disregard the past, but they had a vision that honored the past while building on it by meeting needs now. The church was in the middle of one of the poorest cities in the country, and the city was now full of people of color, immigrants, college students, and younger adults, many of whom were lesbian, gay, bisexual, or transgender—a far cry from the traditional membership of the congregation.

The newcomers, aided by a few sympathetic stalwarts, learned the history of the church, including that it played a role in two significant events affecting racial questions in US history. The first was the *Amistad* incident in 1839 to 1841. The *Amistad* was a slave ship on its way from Sierra Leone to the Caribbean with a full load of African captives intended for sale in the slave markets. The captives mutinied and took control of the ship. Eventually, the ship was captured off the coast of Long Island, and the Africans were taken into custody. Members of several churches in New Haven, Connecticut, came to the aid of the captive Africans and argued all the way to the Supreme Court that these were free people taken against their will and that they should be allowed to return to their homes in Africa. The Supreme Court agreed, and the *Amistad* captives were allowed to return to their homeland. The case was a stunning blow to the institution of slavery in the United States, and the congregation had played a role in that case.

The second case the newcomers learned about was the congregation's role in the Black Panther trials in the early 1970s. The case was a complicated one that involved the murder of a Black Panther member by two other members of the Black Panther Party. The murder took place at the height of the tensions between law enforcement, particularly the FBI, and radical groups such as the Black Panthers. Several members of the party were arrested for the murder, and it became clear that the trial was an excuse to try to break the Black Panthers. Thousands of supporters of the Black Panthers, including many well-known individuals, arrived in New Haven for the trial. Observers widely believed that members of the Panthers would not be able to get a fair trial. Even the chaplain and president of Yale University spoke out against the legal proceedings and the actions of law enforcement in the matter. The congregation played a vital role by housing and feeding many of the protesters and giving sanctuary to members of the Black Panthers not on trial.

Using these two historic moments, times when the congregation reached out in the name of racial justice and freedom, the newcomers were inspired to reach out to the city and to begin working against poverty and other forms of injustice. Such activity created tremendous conflict in the congregation. But at least some members rejoiced that the congregation was back in the business of doing what they believed God was calling them to do to meet the needs of people in the city in their own day and time.

The Anabaptist Witness

These sorts of stories exist in many congregations and denominations. Other stories are perhaps not as dramatic, but nevertheless they are important for understanding that through history, the church has been God's witness to peace, justice, and love. One primary example of this sort of witness is seen in the historic peace churches, such as the Mennonites. The long history of these churches demonstrating a different way of being in the world is full of stories about people willing to live out their witness. These churches that came to be known as "peace churches" are rooted in the Anabaptist tradition. As described earlier, the Anabaptists did not practice infant baptism for both sacramental and political reasons. Their refusal was rooted in their deep commitment to what they understood as the Gospel's call to pacifism. In their very founding, the Anabaptists sought to be churches that transformed the world through reconciliation. Early Anabaptists sought to live as hardworking farmers. They were heavily persecuted for refusing military service and unnerved many people by refusing to defend themselves in the face of persecution and attack. Their witness was one of attempting to live as peaceably as they could in a violent world.

One of the most famous and revered stories from this Anabaptist past is about a Dutch man, Dirk Willems. Willems was arrested for promoting the Anabaptist practice of refusing to baptize infants and encouraging people to choose baptism as young adults. He escaped from prison and in his escape managed to get across a frozen pond. The guards at the prison pursued him once they realized he was gone and also attempted to cross the pond, which had very thin ice. One guard was not so lucky and fell through the ice. Willems, given his faith commitments, could not allow the man to drown and returned to save his captor. He was once again imprisoned, tortured, and finally burned at the stake for his faith. This story is one many people in the various Anabaptist peace traditions tell to illustrate that one must be prepared to live completely a life of peace and reconciliation, even at the risk of death.

As the world shifted into the modern period, the wars of religion in Europe began to pass, and many Anabaptists migrated to North America, some Anabaptists began to take more active roles in helping to relieve hunger and poverty, roles that were often deemed root causes of violence, as well as to take a role in mediating and helping to sort out disputes. The Mennonite Central Committee (MCC), for example, sought to relieve famine across the globe and later partnered with Ten Thousand Villages to serve as a conduit for the sale of goods from poorer countries at fair market prices. Such direct ways of alleviating poverty and hunger also provided service opportunities for conscientious objectors in lieu of military service. Later, MCC would create the Mennonite Conciliation Service to train people to be mediators who try to bring about peaceful resolution of conflicts. This program had direct influence over reconciliation processes in Northern Ireland, South Africa, and many countries in Central America. It also sparked the birth of other centers for peace education, such as the Lombard Mennonite Peace Center in Illinois.

> Anabaptist peace traditions teach that we must be prepared to live completely a life of peace and reconciliation, even at the risk of death.

In other contemporary examples, the work of the Baptist Peace Fellowship of North America (BPFNA) has sought to bring together various groups of Baptists for both education and direct action across the globe. Their efforts are also interfaith while grounded in a Christian ethic true to Baptist faith and tradition. BPFNA has worked with a variety of partners to try to solve various conflicts, including immigration conflicts at the border between the United States and Mexico and conflicts within Baptist congregations around issues of human sexuality. BPFNA has trained hundreds of members of congregations to be peacemakers in their congregations and communities. Their commitment is to bring a culture of peace to any place where there is conflict and injustice.

A Solution for Ghost Ranch

In the 1960s and 1970s, a period of tremendous unrest in the United States and a period of the growth in many liberation movements for people in various racial and ethnic communities, as well as of different gender and sexual orientation, the Presbyterian Church (U.S.A.) found itself embroiled in disputes in northern New Mexico around its retreat and conference center, Ghost Ranch. Ghost Ranch is a 21,000-acre property located near Abiquiú, New Mexico. The area is rich in history that involves Native Americans, Hispanics, and Anglo-Europeans. Home to the artist Georgia O'Keeffe for many years, Ghost Ranch is an oasis for many now, but when the Presbyterian Church purchased the land, there was a great deal of tension between local ranchers, most of whom were Hispanic and Native American, and the Anglos who owned the ranch. There were several threats to occupy and take over the ranch and reclaim it for the locals. The director of the ranch at the time, the Rev. Jim Hall, not only wanted to preserve the property for the Presbyterians—he also cared deeply for the local people and wanted a good working relationship with the local community, including its many local employees. Hall was known for often saying that "he did not want Ghost Ranch to be just for *Presbyterian* cows."[4]

> Our history demonstrates that conflict has always been present in the church and that we have resources for addressing it.

The ranch opened its lands to local ranchers and its recreational facilities to local children. Local artists were invited to sell their work to ranch guests, a practice that continues to this day. The ranch became a partner in supporting local endeavors and concerns, especially when the US Army Corps of Engineers began to seize land, including some of the ranch, to build a dam over the nearby Chama River. While unsuccessful in stopping the project, which was designed to provide water to Albuquerque while bypassing the town of Abiquiú, the ranch agreed to give up more land so that Abiquiú could have water rights as well. All of these practices were more than ways to build good relationships with the local community. They were deeply rooted in a faith conviction for justice and peaceful relationships.

In June 1969, the ranch got word that a local Hispanic activist and his followers intended to take over the ranch property and reclaim it for Hispanic peoples. When they arrived, Hall and the staff welcomed them and offered them refreshments. Many local people came to stand with the ranch, and after a few speeches and conversation, the protestors left and didn't return. The ranch to this day continues its policies of local involvement and support.

The history of the church demonstrates that conflict is natural and normal in the life of the church as a whole and in individual congregations. It also offers us examples of how the church has handled conflict poorly as well as how the church has helped to resolve or even prevent conflict—examples from which we can learn. The church has also been a participant in relieving suffering and providing sanctuary in the midst of conflict. Finally, our history demonstrates that conflict has always been present in the church and that we have resources for addressing it.

Reframing Our Perspective: The Role of the Holy Spirit

The third resource for rethinking change and conflict in the church is a theology of the Holy Spirit and of the Spirit's work. As faith communities, congregations are called into existence by God and are sustained by God's guidance through the Holy Spirit. The process of discerning the ongoing presence of the Spirit, growing in faith, determining the mission that the Spirit of God is leading a congregation toward, and being a prophetic and faithful witness requires careful and attentive work. Discernment means understanding that different people in the congregation will be at different places in their individual journeys of faith and therefore see things differently. Members of congregations have different life experiences, as well. The Spirit does not offer conflicting messages, but rather the Spirit speaks to each of us where we are in our life journey, and we therefore understand situations and decisions based on where we are.

Spirit-Led Conflict?

As stated earlier, conflict is a normal and natural part of life in the community of faith. Every congregation will experience conflict, but conflict may consist of more than disagreements among people. Conflict may, in fact, be a sign of the Holy Spirit's activity. The Holy Spirit is a guide, a teacher, and a provoker. The Holy Spirit serves to inspire, nudge, and push us as individuals and congregations to think and act differently.

One congregation that had been experiencing a slow and steady decline finally had its difficulties come to a head with the resignation of the beloved youth minister over an affair with someone outside the congregation. The aftermath of the resignation saw the congregation split into bitter factions focused on the ministries of the two remaining copastors. Each faction brought a different perspective about what was wrong with the copastors and by extension the congregation. Those who were older and particularly those who cared for homebound members were distressed that the pastors spent little time visiting them. Their perspective was that home visitation was a primary task of a pastor. Middle-aged members of the congregation who served on the committees and council were concerned about the lack of leadership and administrative organization.

> Conflict may be a sign of the Holy Spirit's activity. The Holy Spirit is a guide, a teacher, and a provoker. The Holy Spirit serves to inspire, nudge, and push us as individuals and congregations to think and act differently.

Worship was another dividing line. The deacons, who had primary responsibility for worship, were unhappy with the way worship was being handled. They complained bitterly about the problems with preaching, prayer styles, and other elements of the service. They wanted to participate more in planning and wanted the service to feel "the way it used to feel," but no one quite knew what that meant. The point they could agree on was that worship was lackluster and poorly executed. The evidence they raised was low attendance and the fact that a breakaway group offered an alternative worship service between the traditional services that was personal and focused on the life experience of those who attended. This group included a large number of people who had recently divorced or been through some other personal trauma.

Finally, a group of parents with young children were actually happy with the pastors. They felt their children and they as young parents were cared for. These factions came from different life experiences and faith journeys that informed each group what church was supposed to be about and how a pastor should address to their concerns. These differences led to squabbling over the priorities for pastoral ministry and the congregation as a whole—a recipe for conflict.

Many members believed in retrospect that while there were real differences in perspectives in the congregation, the Holy Spirit was at work, stirring up the conflict to get the congregation moving. The congregation had become complacent and willing to tolerate a slow decline in a large church with wonderful resources. The conflict occurred at a point that the congregation could still reverse the malaise and become the dynamic, cutting-edge faith community it had once been. The conflict was painful and difficult, but by following the lead of the Holy Spirit, the congregation moved beyond mediocrity. Perhaps the perfect storm of conflict was coincidence, but as people of faith, the congregation saw it as the Spirit's leading.

> The Spirit is moving in the church today, and the central question is whether we are willing and courageous enough to discern that movement and take our cues from it regarding change in the church.

The Way of the Spirit

The Scriptures affirm that the Spirit is beyond human control and with divine agency goes and comes where it will. Comparing the Spirit to the wind Jesus said, "The wind blows where it chooses, and you hear the sound of it, but you do not know where it comes from or where it goes. So it is with everyone who is born of the Spirit" (John 3:8).

The Holy Spirit is credited with leading Jesus into the wilderness. The Spirit brings dreams and visions. The Holy Spirit sparks the speaking in tongues on Pentecost. These examples from Scripture tend to make most churches nervous, because the Spirit cannot be controlled, instigating and provoking change—and, by extension, conflict.

A quote attributed to German theologian Jürgen Moltmann says, "Show me a church where there is no conflict, and I will show you a church where the Holy Spirit does not reside."[5] This statement is quite apt, helping us to reframe our perspective on conflict. The Spirit is moving in the church today, and the central question is whether we are willing and courageous enough to discern that movement and take our cues from it regarding change in the church. If conflict can be a sign of the Spirit's movement in the church, then to treat conflict as a problem, instead of a sign, can thwart the movement of the Spirit and cause us to miss the message.

Any number of the examples discussed in this chapter offer an opportunity to see the hand of the Holy Spirit at work. In the "Happy + Nice" church at the beginning of the chapter, the Holy Spirit was present in the urging of the church's leaders to finally get to the bottom of the conflict they repeatedly experienced. The Holy Spirit could also been seen in the aftermath of the interviews as the church began to wrestle with the fact that God wasn't in the equation. There was a deep sense amongst the leaders of the congregation that they were being led to do what they were doing. They didn't necessarily understand it, but they knew they were supposed to continue the exploration and conversations. As an observer of their process, I heard repeatedly that they "just knew" that they were called to do what they were doing. "Just knowing" can be a real sign of the Spirit's leading. The letter to the Romans states: "Likewise the Spirit helps us in our weakness; for we do not know how to pray as we ought, but that very Spirit intercedes with sighs too deep for words" (Romans 8:26).

> The measure of the church's mission may be seen most clearly in the way it handles conflict and seeks to learn from it, heal from it, and discern from it.

The congregation that built the housing complex on its property saw the leading of the Holy Spirit in every aspect of that project. As people looked back over the entire process, from conception to completion, they credited the Holy Spirit for all aspects. The idea to do something different with the piece of property and the brainstorming about what could be done were infused with an imagination the congregation had not displayed for a long time. Building relationships with partners in the affordable housing community and with the city made the dream become reality. And they had the courage to face neighborhood opposition and to work at building relationships with new neighbors who were from a different culture and faith tradition. Every step they felt the leading of God through the Holy Spirit.

The business of the church is to be about God's business. And a significant portion of God's business is reconciliation, as demonstrated in the life, death, and resurrection of Jesus Christ. Our role in that business is to be open to and willing to follow the lead of the Holy Spirit, who makes us the concrete and visible hands of God. The measure of the church's mission may be seen most clearly in the way it handles conflict and seeks to learn from it, heal from it, and discern from it.

Reflecting on Your Congregation . . .

1. Consider a conflict that your congregation has experienced.

   Did you consider Scripture, tradition, or the Holy Spirit as resources for reframing the conflict?

   If so, how did you do that?

   If you did not consider those resources in the conflict, how might they help you now to look back and reconsider the conflict in light of Scripture? Tradition? The Holy Spirit?

2. What stories of courage in conflict within your congregation or in the wider community are part of your congregation's history?

   How might these help to shape a new understanding of conflict for your congregation?

3. Are particular Scripture passages important to your congregation when a conflict arises? If so, how are these used?

4. What role does the Holy Spirit play in sermons and conversations in your congregation?

5. How might you strengthen your own theology of the Holy Spirit?

Why Is Change
So Difficult?

Understanding and Managing the
Process of Transformation

We all know that change is a natural part of life. Without change we would stagnate and die. We age, and as we age our bodies adapt to realities we never dreamed of coping with when we were younger. Organizations age as well and in their aging have to contend with a variety of internal and external issues. The church is no different. The world, our culture, and our society change at a rapid pace, and for the church to truly be the church, we must be prepared to live in and respond to the changes. Churches that know how to read the changes around them and respond appropriately and in a timely way are able to adapt, grow, and flourish. Congregations that deny societal and cultural shifts and become virtual museums to an earlier time and place, as well as congregations that constantly say no to the changes around them, typically wither and die.

Common Sources for Change in the Church

Congregations face many issues that factor into the changes present today. Often these factors are both sources for change and sources of conflict. The changes can force conflict because people are unhappy with the various changes taking place in the culture or within the congregation. Their displaced unhappiness can lead to conflict because there is no way to control the situation and congregations are forced to deal with changes they would prefer not to have happen.

Aging or Declining Membership

Many congregations are in decline, and one of the common approaches to dealing with it is denial. The majority of mainline Protestant denominations and congregations—and even many evangelical and Roman Catholic congregations—have experienced a loss of members and with that a loss of money, prestige, and power in our society. For example, according to the Presbyterian Church (U.S.A.) General Assembly Mission Council, in 2000 the denomination had over 2.5 million members. Over the past decade the denomination has lost over 20 percent of its membership.[1] This decline is occurring in part because North American culture is no longer religious. That is, most people do not claim formal, institutional church affiliation. The culture is clearly post-Christian despite pockets where Christianity still seems dominant. According to the Pew Research Religion and Public Life Project, 78.4 percent of Americans self-identify as Christian.[2] While these people are still a majority of the population, we need to keep in mind that self-identifying and actually participating are two different things. In another study by the Public Religion Research Institute, only 31 percent of Americans report attending worship services.[3] Yet churches tend to act like we still have significant influence in our society, choosing to deny our lack of prestige and power and attempting to maintain business as usual.

> Churches that know how to read the changes around them and respond appropriately and in a timely way are able to adapt, grow, and flourish.

Instead of denying the decline, some churches accept the declining membership and choose to do nothing about it, seemingly saying, *We will hang in there until we can bury each other, and the last one out just needs to turn off the lights.* This was the case with one church I worked with. The pastor told me their decline was inevitable, and the congregation was interested only in keeping going long enough to bury all current members. Membership was dwindling rapidly. I tried to recruit them for a revitalization program, and there was absolutely no interest.

Another small and declining congregation I knew actually had substantial financial resources and had decided to build a new building. The building wasn't designed for planned outreach, new programs, or anything resembling revitalization and growth. The members had worked up a chart indicating their best guesses for how much time would pass before each person could no longer climb the steep steps into the old building for worship, and they figured they needed a new and accessible building to accommodate themselves. They were also worried about getting caskets up and down the steps of the old building. They had no vision, no sense of responsibility for mission, and no willingness to consider that God might have something different in mind for them.

Some congregations recognize decline and start grasping at every trick, every strategy, every idea we think might be a life raft, without substantively changing the congregation and how we operate, worship, and practice community together. Usually these congregations experience a great deal of conflict over which life raft to cling to. There is no real discernment about our mission or what ministry God might be calling us to or what church means in this day and age. We turn to experts or megachurch pastors and adopt their formulas and recipes for success, failing to realize that our context will not support a megachurch model or that we will have to fundamentally change who and what we are as a church to attract newcomers. We often see technology as the key to salvation. We think, *If we only had a website (or a better website) or a great Facebook page, we could be raking in visitors and potential new members.*

> Some congregations recognize decline and start grasping at every trick, every strategy, every idea we think might be a life raft, without substantively changing the congregation and how we operate, worship, and practice community together.

Finally, some congregations determine that the problem is not with the congregation but with the pastor. As a result, the pastor is harassed, put under extreme pressure, and, in some cases, dismissed in our attempt to ensure the congregation survives. The pastor may or may not have been a primary reason for the decline but becomes the sacrificial lamb as we become increasingly desperate to save the church. Of course, any debate over the retention of the pastor creates conflict. People line up for or against the pastor, and these divisions are usually bitter and result in the loss of more members, especially if the pastor leaves.

Clashes with Changing Society

Another common change going on in many congregations is the clash with modern culture. One issue putting many congregations at odds with the culture around them is that, increasingly, marriage between two people of the same gender is legal. These changes in the law have thrown many congregations into a quandary about how to respond if a lesbian or gay couple approaches them. The law does not require churches to perform marriage ceremonies for same-gender couples, but congregations become embroiled in conflict internally over whether we should or shouldn't. Congregations also worry about how our either refusing to or agreeing to do a wedding will affect our reputation in the community.

In some congregations, deliberations about how to respond to cultural change have become a slugfest between two camps. No one is comfortable about the way things go in the conversation, but emotions, hyperbole, and sound bites win the day. Often congregations are left bitterly divided. Other congregations find ways to have thoughtful conversation that result in a shared decision. Others leave the decision up to the pastor, and then the pastor is left wondering how it will affect her ministry and tenure at the church.

Pastoral Transition

A shift in pastoral leadership brings changes through grieving the loss of a pastor or relief at the departure of a pastor, the style of the interim pastor and/or the new pastor, and changes in membership as some members leave and others join. Congregations may have the option of working with an intentional interim to ease the process, but with or without an interim pastor, change is thrust upon the congregation. We must find ways to adapt, attend to the grieving process as we let go of the former pastor, and look seriously at the key elements of pastoral transition. These tasks are critical to receiving a new pastor and ensuring a successful pastorate. These elements are:

- Coming to terms with the congregation's history
- Discerning the congregation's purpose and identity

- Initiating leadership change and development in lay and staff leadership
- Reaffirming community and denominational ties
- Committing to new leadership, a new ministry, and a new future

If these tasks are not accomplished, then our ability to change and adapt to new pastoral leadership is severely weakened. This is where an intentional interim can be quite helpful. Unfortunately, some congregations that could have worked with an intentional interim have rushed the process and gotten a new pastor in as quickly as possible, without taking time to work through the five tasks. Even in denominational systems where judicatory officials periodically appoint pastors to congregations, so such changes are to be expected, we still need to address all of the implications of the former pastor's departure and the possibilities a new pastor brings.

The Path of Change

We generally think change happens when we start at point A and make a leap to point B. This is the "gap model" of change; we see a change and assume that a person or an organization jumped across the gap in one leap. What we fail to see are all of the steps and processes in between.

In fact, change can be better viewed as the way we sail a boat. If we want to go from the pier or the shore to a point on the horizon, we do not aim the boat at the far-distant point and head straight for it. If we are trying to sail into the wind, such a strategy is sure to put us off-course and even in danger. Rather, we tack to aim at a point that puts us at an angle to the wind, and then tack to another point and so forth. The course is a zigzag, to be sure, but it gets us where we intend to go.

Researcher, teacher, and author Everett M. Rogers in his groundbreaking book *Diffusion of Innovations* argues that whenever people or organizations make changes, the path of that change rarely jumps from A to B in one leap.

As in tacking, people go through stages of change. Each stage allows us to establish some equilibrium and to adjust before moving to the next stage in the change process. Rogers identifies five stages we go through to make a change or adopt an innovation:

1. Awareness of the possibility of change through knowledge
2. Persuasion to take an interest in exploring this new possibility

3. Evaluation of the old ways and the new possibility; and decision to pursue
4. Implementation, which includes an evaluation trial period
5. Acceptance or confirmation of the change[4]

Gap models of change say we go from awareness to acceptance, but Rogers argues that the steps in between are vital to successful and positively received change.

According to Rogers, people on the path of change go through the five stages in different ways and at different rates of speed. He lists five categories of individuals and the usual percentage of a group that each category comprises.

Innovators or "the brave"—These folks are enthusiastic about finding and implementing new ideas. They make up about 2.5 percent of the group.

Early adopters or "the respectable"—These people are able to quickly assess the possibilities in change and comfortably adapt to change. They are also well respected in the organization and make up about 1.5 percent of the group.

Early majority or "the thoughtful"—These individuals listen carefully to the early adopters but take more time to evaluate and decide. They make up about 34 percent of an organization.

Late majority or "the skeptical"—These people are, as the name suggests, skeptical of change. They will eventually go along but not until the change is proven to be a success. They make up about 34 percent of the organization.

Laggards or "the traditional"—These people are usually not going to change. If they do change, it takes quite a while for them to do so. The term "laggards" may seem judgmental, but it is accurate. They make up about 16 percent of the organization.[5]

Often when I work with congregations facing change, I observe people smiling as I describe each category. They know almost immediately who they can assign to each category.

Note, however, that although we may perceive a person to consistently be in the late majority or even laggard group, it is possible for people to be in different categories depending on the change at hand.

We also need to be careful not to see late majority or laggard folks as hopeless cases who will wind up leaving if they do not agree with the congregation's decision. It is possible for people to be resigned to the change, even if they are not in favor of it, and to remain an important part of the congregation. An elderly gentleman in one congregation I worked with still, many years after a decision had been made, disagreed with his church's choice to welcome LGBTQ people. He had been passionate in his opposition at the time the decision was being considered but he did not act out, bully, or threaten to leave the congregation if he didn't get his way. One day, I asked him why he had stayed at the church even though he didn't agree with the decision. He replied that it was his church, and his disagreeing was no reason to leave. "You don't always get your way," he reminded me. He added that it was important to him that he had been heard and respected even though he wasn't with the majority. He felt he could remain active and good friends with people in the church because his opposition was never demeaned or disrespected. In fact, he was taken seriously.

Change done well allows for a wide variety of opinions in an environment where everyone is heard, respected, and treated well. Such change happens when the congregation creates safe and hospitable space. Tough decisions need not be handled in an ugly manner. Changing congregations might experience tension and disagreement, but that does not mean people need to be ignored, shut down, or disrespected in the conversation and deliberation. If we truly are to be a reconciling community carrying out Christ's charge to us, then we must also be a community that seeks peace and harmony and still honors the diversity of opinion within our midst.

The Flavors of Change

When leading a congregation through change, we must understand what sort of change we are dealing with and what kind of leadership is required to address it. Here, the work of leadership expert Ronald A. Heifetz is particularly helpful. In *The Practice of Adaptive Leadership*, Heifetz, along with his colleagues Alexander Grashow and Marty Linsky, offers a number of tactics to help leaders identify the various kinds of change (or, in Heifetz's language, "challenges") and the skills and strategies required to manage them.

Heifetz identifies three kinds of challenges that many organizations face today. For each type of challenge, he explains how problems are defined, how solutions are most effectively arrived at, and where the work is to be done. These challenges imply change of one sort or the other when they are responded to in an organization.

Technical Challenges

We know we are dealing with a technical challenge when the problem is easy to define and we already know the solution. The roof needs to be replaced. The furnace is no longer working. The church needs to set up a database or a website. These are clearly defined challenges for church leaders. There is little debate about what the issue is, and the solutions are clear. We need a new roof or furnace. We need to purchase software for a database. We need a platform for the website. To meet these solutions, we turn to someone who is an expert on roofing or furnaces or databases or building websites. Problem solved. Challenge met.

Adaptive Challenges

We face an adaptive challenge when we cannot easily define the problem or identify the solution. We know something is wrong or not working, but we don't understand what the real issue is, so we can't address it.

For instance, many congregations struggle to understand why our pews are getting emptier and what can be done about it. This is an adaptive challenge. To define the issue requires we listen carefully to those most affected by the adaptive challenge and learn from them; and only then do we move to find a solution.

Those most affected are those who hold a stake in the future of a congregation. They are important sources of valuable insight. This includes those within the congregation already, but also potential members or ministry partners. The founders of many megachurches, in seeking to attract people to come to church who were not invested in belonging to a church, began their work by going out into the neighborhood and listening to and learning from those who were there. They asked, *Do you go to church? If so, why? If not, why not? What would you want in a church if you decided to go?*

Addressing adaptive challenges also requires learning to listen inside the church. We know we need to change many aspects of congregations, but we may not want to acknowledge the changes needed, so we avoid listening for them. Deep inside, many of us know things need to change in a major way. But we fear that such change will negate what we have known all our lives or will somehow take away our sense of ownership and power in the church. We want to see membership numbers rise but we are afraid to change what we know and possibly lose control of "our" church. "For those who want to save their life will lose it, and those who lose their life for my sake will find it" (Matthew 16:25). Is the mission of the church to comfort its members or to serve the realm of God?

> Change done well allows for a wide variety of opinions in an environment where everyone is heard, respected, and treated well.

I consulted with a church that was concerned it was dying. They could afford only a part-time pastor, and although a few new people had joined the church, from what I could determine, newcomers were welcomed only as long as they didn't want any changes to the way things had always been done. For instance, the congregation still used a hymnal published in 1941 by a denomination the congregation no longer belonged to. The hymns were quite old and, while in English, used language that seemed antiquated and out of touch with contemporary theology and society. Any attempt to adopt a new hymnal was firmly rebuffed by the longtime members, because the old hymnal connected the congregation to its immigrant roots. It was familiar and comforting to the longtime members even if the language seemed strange to the newcomers.

As we talked, I realized the members' primary concern was that even their own children and grandchildren—let alone their neighbors, friends, and strangers—weren't interested in coming to church. I asked them what would have to happen to attract their children and grandchildren back to church. "Oh, a whole lot would have to change," was the reply. We went on to explore what those changes might look like. For these longtime and faithful members to realize that they themselves might be the reason the congregation couldn't attract new members was painful. The solution would have required them to become willing to change.

Adaptive challenges are often demanding. They push us out of our comfort zones and move us toward solutions that can take us into new territory. Making the change is a struggle, and it definitely means we can't go back to business as usual. If, however, we do the hard work of listening and learning, and we make the changes demanded of us, we will find the rewards wonderful, even as they push us to act in new ways.

Technical and Adaptive Challenges

The third kind of challenge is a mix of the first two. These challenges have both a technical and an adaptive component. Usually, in this case, the issue at hand is fairly clearly defined but the solution requires us to learn and listen carefully to both those who are experts and those who have a stake in the congregation. This requires more finesse for leaders. And it requires us to spend more time talking with experts and those who are stakeholders in the system.

Changing the style of the worship service from traditional to one that might appeal to younger people is an example of a mixed challenge. The solution will involve gathering information from musicians, experts in using multimedia and web-based worship aids, and others who know more about contemporary worship. It will require conversations with both current members of the congregation and those who are not currently members but might be interested in the congregation. This information we gather from experts and stakeholders can be used to develop a strategy for the change. The change will not necessarily occur overnight, although it might. Or it could require multiple changes over a longer period of time. The congregation can adjust, and revisions to the original plan can be made as the worship patterns are altered.

> We must listen carefully to those most affected by the challenge and learn from them; and only then do we move to find a solution.

One of the congregations I served wrestled with the style of its service. Wanting to appeal to people in the congregation with both preferences, leaders designed a mixed service that combined the best elements of both

styles. Any given service might include a traditional organ prelude followed by a call to worship using a contemporary call-and-response song
accompanied by the piano, a Bach chorale by the choir, and a jazz offer-
tory on the piano. The staff worked hard to make eclectic elements work
together and as a result were able to unite rather than divide the congregation through worship. The blended service also made more efficient use
of staff members' time, as they had to prepare for one only service each
weekend.

Rogers's and Heifetz's theories give us a good grounding for understanding how to plan for and manage change. Rogers helps us anticipate
the range of responses to change that we will
likely encounter. Heifetz and his coauthors
propose developing a strategy to deal with
the challenges that change brings to an organization. A strong strategy allows for taking
risks and experimenting, and yet does not
throw out the past and tradition. It recognizes that the more diverse an organization
is, the more able it is to adapt and change. It
recognizes that transformation doesn't happen overnight and that change will reorga-
nize at least some of the organization's
DNA.[6]

The leaders who develop and guide a
change strategy must be adaptive as well. As
Heifetz and his colleagues observe, "Adaptive leadership is the practice of
mobilizing people to tackle tough challenges and thrive."[7] It is grounded
in the realities of today's world and the challenges of the change we face.

> A strong strategy allows for taking risks and experimenting, and yet does not throw out the past and tradition. It recognizes that the more diverse an organization is, the more able it is to adapt and change.

Planning for Change

Carefully thought-through change is crucial for congregations. Rogers and
Heifetz are helpful guides for leaders planning a strategy for change.

Change generally comes about in one of three ways. First, a problem
presents itself—the roof is leaking and it needs to be fixed. Second, a person or small group of people brings an idea forward. These are usually the

innovators, in Rogers's terminology. New ideas can range from a new way to do Christian education to a mission project reaching out into the wider community to a new way of doing stewardship or new member development. A new idea is something that will change the status quo, even if slightly, and move the congregation to work together in new ways. And finally, there are changes that no one can predict. An extreme example is the death of a pastor. We will return to the third avenue of change later in this chapter.

Beginning with Heifetz, you need to determine what sort of change your congregation is dealing with. Are you looking at a technical change, adaptive change, or a combination of the two? If the change is technical, then the process is fairly straightforward. Leaders must identify the issue and then identify an authority or authorities to help create the solution. Once this is done, the solution can be implemented. The church building needs a new roof. Bids are collected from reputable contractors. The job is awarded to a contractor, and the roof is replaced. Change is managed with relatively little angst or conflict.

But what if this same roofing problem becomes an issue because the congregation has no money to repair the roof? This moves the change closer to the combined change category. It is now both technical and adaptive, as leaders must address the financial concerns. From the technical perspective, leaders still need to get bids from reputable contractors and explore loan possibilities. These technical challenges may imply others: Is a loan the best way to move forward? How is the church investing its money, and what financial and theological principles are being used to govern the financial resources of the church? These are technical questions.

However, the financial concerns imply the possibility of adaptive change, such as questions about stewardship and giving patterns, which are crucial for the long-term viability of the congregation. And those questions, adaptive in nature, may in turn raise further questions about church growth. Leaders cannot bid those jobs out to a contractor who will provide a solution. Consultants can be helpful, and resources are available, but experts can take a congregation only so far. The congregation's members will need to have a serious conversation with one another and discern and pray together about where God might be leading them in this process.

Other changes are purely adaptive for a congregation. For instance, the decision to welcome LGBTQ people is a tough one for many congregations. This idea is usually proposed by a person or a few people who are interested in seeing this change in the congregation. The change has many facets and carries the potential for great division in a congregation. Members fear the implications of such a decision and offer a wide variety of opinions, laden with emotion, as to whether such a decision is the right one. Such a change opens the door to differing interpretations of Scripture and understandings of morality. It taps into people's experiences with sexuality and gay and lesbian people. It also opens the door for stereotypes and falsehoods about homosexuality to be put forth as facts. It is not a subject that people are neutral about. It is not a change to be undertaken lightly—and yet it is not a change that needs to be as scary as many congregational leaders make it out to be.

Developing a Proposal for Change

How might we plan a strategy for a change that is purely adaptive? The process Rogers lays out begins with the innovators who bring forth the idea. Let us assume a small group of congregational members has approached the pastor about the possibility of welcoming LGBTQ people into the congregation. Let us also assume that the pastor does not shut down the conversation immediately. What are the next steps?

The first step is for the pastor and the small group of innovators to assess the readiness of the congregation to have a discussion about the change. Do members share an understanding of how the church interprets Scripture? In the past, how has the church dealt with difficult issues, such as the ordination of women? If the church has not handled other so-called controversial issues well, that has implications for how it will handle this one. How has the church dealt with conflict in the past? These are some of the areas that need to be considered in planning a strategy.

The second step is to identify members and lay leaders who might be early adopters of this change. They need to be brought on board early to support a decision to even take up the topic for congregational discernment. Many churches make the mistake of immediately taking an idea to the council, board, or other governing body without preparation. Conversations that are sprung with no preparation on leaders, whether with the governing board or the congregation, are never helpful and usually serve to end the conversation before it begins. This result is often accompanied by hard feelings and creates a scar that makes future conversations more difficult.

By identifying the early adopters and seeking their counsel early on, the innovators recruit solid and respected allies for a conversation. This does not imply that becoming a welcoming congregation is guaranteed, but rather increases the likelihood of a successful conversation about becoming welcoming. The early adopters will have important insights into other members' thoughts and feelings on the issue. Innovators tend to be passionate about their ideas, which often makes it difficult for them to accurately gauge the congregation's receptivity. Innovators need the early adopters to temper their passion and design a reasonable and thoughtful way to proceed.

The third step is to clearly define the role of the pastor in the strategy for change. While the pastor will have opinions about the issue, it is crucial that the pastor stay out of a leadership role as the congregation makes the decision. The pastor's leadership role is to provide spiritual counsel to all

First Steps Toward Change

1. With the pastor and small group of innovators, assess the readiness of the congregation to have a discussion and evaluate how the church has dealt with change in the past.

2. Identify members and lay leaders who might be early adopters of this change. Seek to bring them on board before approaching a church council or other governing body.

3. Clearly define the role of the pastor, who should be there to provide spiritual counsel to all and to support the conversation.

4. Design a proposal for the church's leaders, rather than the whole congregation, defining the issue at hand but not dictating an outcome for discernment.

and to support the conversation. This does not mean the pastor cannot or should not make known her thoughts and feelings on the issue, but the pastor must also let go of the outcome and make clear to members that the decision rests with the congregation. This is a difficult role for a pastor, but the alternative is for the pastor to become a target in a highly charged conversation, and as a target, to become a distraction to the hard work of deep conversation. If becoming welcoming is seen as the pastor's pet project, then that opens the door for people to focus on the pastor and not the issue. It is a way of derailing the discernment process.

Once these three steps have been taken, the small group of innovators and early adopters, minus the pastor (but keeping the pastor informed), is ready to design a proposal for the church's leaders. Facilitators of change recommend that the council or other governing body first discern whether to have a congregational conversation, rather than approaching the congregation as a whole. A thoughtful conversation with the governing body is a way of testing out the thoughts and feelings of the larger congregation on the topic of welcoming. The small group of leaders will discover whether they can move forward and what issues will arise in the congregation if the conversation occurs. The support of the governing body will bode well for continued conversation. The lack of support may either end the conversation or force the planning group to rethink its strategy.

> An initial proposal needs to be clear and relatively short: Here is the issue. Here is why it is important. Here is how we will go about discerning.

When creating an initial proposal, the planning group needs to define the issue at hand but not dictate an outcome for the discernment. They can be clear with members about where individuals in the planning group stand, but they also need to be clear that implementing their preferences is not a foregone conclusion. If congregational members believe they are not free to make a decision, then they will reject the process or try to sabotage it. This reaction is not a mature one, but it is a very human one.

The initial proposal should define the issue, explain why the congregation should discuss and make a decision about it, and propose a way to go about having a conversation. The proposal needs to be clear and relatively short: Here is the issue. Here is why it is important. Here is how we will go about discerning. On the last point, planners should draw on their assessment of the congregation's readiness for the conversation. In the case of a decision about welcoming LGBTQ people, if the congregation does not have a clear, shared understanding of how to interpret Scripture, the strategy may start with a series of adult education sessions and sermons on Scripture in general before ever taking up a specific issue like human sexuality. I know of a congregation that offered an adult version of the human sexuality curriculum used with middle-school children to help people become comfortable talking about human sexuality in general, then specifically individual sexuality.

Providing educational sessions, facilitated small-group conversations, films, sermons, and other means of information, as well as creating safe settings for conversation are all helpful to a discernment process. Leaders should not set up debates between opposing sides. Usually debates just ramp up emotions, incite anger, and encourage people to take sides. True discernment opens the door for congregational members to consider issues thoughtfully, prayerfully, and carefully. Planners should resist the temptation to follow the wider culture in the tendency to demean others' points of view. Remember the story told earlier of the gentleman who said he did not agree with the decision to become welcoming but appreciated being heard and respected for his opinion.

Finding creative ways to open up conversation allows congregations to consider an issue from a different point of view and reflect on the issue. Such creative channels can lower anxiety and ease people into considering a point of view they would not normally adopt. One congregation I was part of created a reader's theater of stories from congregational members about becoming welcoming and what it meant to them. Members were invited to submit short reflections on their

> True discernment opens the door for congregational members to consider issues thoughtfully, prayerfully, and carefully. We must resist the temptation to follow the wider culture in the tendency to demean others' points of view.

thoughts on becoming welcoming. The stories were not submitted anonymously, but they were treated as confidential by the member collecting them, and those who submitted stories were not identified by name when the stories were presented. A member of the church who was gifted in theater edited the reflections, and a number of talented reader-actors in the congregation presented the edited reflections as a theater piece at Sunday morning worship in place of the sermon. The actors did not read their own reflections, if they had submitted any, and the congregation was told that fact. The congregation was also told that everything presented came from members of the congregation. Listeners were moved to hear stories about members who had come out, parents who were gay, or congregants who had brothers, sisters, uncles, or cousins who were gay and important in their lives. The theater presented a human face to the issue rather than just scriptural, scientific, or cultural understandings of human sexuality.

As many members of the congregation as possible should be engaged in the education and conversation. Methods could include short information pieces as part of worship or meetings of every group in the church. Another possibility is for the planning team to facilitate conversation in existing church groups, such as the women's fellowship or the men's breakfast club, as well as open conversations that are "y'all come." The process may move quickly or slowly, but it must continue to move toward some sort of resolution.

The date for a resolution can be predetermined or it can be flexible. The advantage of a preset date is that people know the process is a defined one that has an end. The disadvantage of a preset date is it may force a decision before people are ready to make one. A flexible ending for a decision-making process has the advantage of giving the planning team and congregational leadership the freedom to determine when people are ready to make a decision. The disadvantage is that decisions can be put off indefinitely, causing the congregation to become discouraged and weary of the process.

Hints for Success

In designing a strategy for change, the question always arises as to how to deal with those who are not in favor of change or who try to sabotage the process. When considering strategies for change, here are some important hints for success:

Don't design the process for the laggards or the late adopters. This is a common mistake. The laggards are not going to change, and focusing on convincing them will only slow the process down or end it altogether. Some of the late adopters will come along, but they usually do so long after the change occurs and is well accepted.

I am reminded of a woman in a congregation who was adamant that the congregation would never welcome "those people," meaning LGBTQ people. She fought the process, and then one day when it was clear almost everyone else was moving forward, she decided to absent herself, so she would not detract from the process. She had moved from laggard to late adopter. Much later, the pastor found her sitting at a potluck with a gay male couple who were visiting the church for the first time. She was telling them how wonderful it was to have them as guests and that she hoped they would come back. She got to the party late, but she got there nonetheless. The process didn't wait for her to catch up, however.

Recognize that you are looking for innovators to get your process moving and to influence the early adopters. Once you have the innovators and early adopters on board, change will happen if you attend to it. The tipping point for change is usually around 20 percent. Together these two groups make up 16 percent of a community, and all they need to do is move a few members of the early majority on board, and change is well on its way. The innovators and early adopters will sway those in the middle, building up the early majority. From there you are able to make change against the resistance of the laggards and even some of the late adopters.

Encourage and support innovators and early adopters in being change agents. Inviting early adopters to meet with others one-on-one or in small groups is helpful. Ensuring early adopters have the information and tools they need to help bring about change is essential. Thanking the early adopters for their work in bringing about change is also important.

Laggards can be resilient, but remember that they are a small percentage. They will sound like they are the majority. They are not. You should hear them, but do not let them control the process. And do not delay decision making hoping they will come around, because a decision will never be made if you wait for everyone to agree.

Do not be afraid of losing members. This is a major stumbling block for many congregations. We want to keep everyone. Sometimes people cannot go where the congregation feels led to go, and trying to keep them can stymie the congregation's mission and encourage their group to work against the congregation. People leave churches for a multitude of reasons. Better to bless people and encourage them to find a congregation that suits their views and needs than try to retain people who do not support the mission of the congregation.

Pastors must be present to all people in the process of change, especially those who are most uncertain or most against a decision under consideration. Pastoral care is one way of hearing and respecting people. Pastors are often tempted to shy away from people who are exhibiting unpleasant behavior, but this is a time when pastoral presence is needed more than ever. Ministering in such circumstances is not easy and people may not accept pastoral outreach, but pastors must make the effort.

Unanticipated Change

Sometimes change in the life of the congregation is unforeseen. The pastor or a strong leader dies, leaving a void in leadership. Events such as the shock and horror of 9/11 happen in the wider world. The church building is destroyed by fire, an earthquake, or other natural disaster. A leader is diagnosed with a serious illness. A longtime trusted leader is arrested for embezzlement of church funds or for being a sexual predator of children. The list goes on and on. Change happens and will keep happening despite our best efforts to control things.

Such unanticipated events can throw a congregation into a tailspin. Emotions are swirling and difficult to address. People are living with shock, grief, anger, and myriad other emotions. Life in the congregation will be chaotic no matter what is done to address the chaos. Despite our own emotions, leaders must find a way to become a calm, nonanxious presence in the midst of tragedy or malfeasance (more on this in chapter 4). Once we do, the process of managing change can unfold. The more these skills in change management are practiced before crisis, the more easily they can be exercised in crisis.

The same questions need to be asked in crises as in calmer periods of the congregation's life:

1. Who are your idea people, the innovators? What gifts can they bring to the situation to begin to address the problems and develop a strategy?
2. Are you dealing with a technical challenge, an adaptive challenge, or both?
3. Who are the early adopters to bring on board with the innovators to begin to organize for change?
4. How can you develop your strategy and move forward?

Bring in experts, if needed. Organize conversation among stakeholders within and beyond the congregation. Implement the strategy and move toward a decision, proceeding prayerfully and thoughtfully.

Take the example of a congregation whose historic church building burnt to the ground in a tragic fire after a piece of equipment a workman left turned on caught fire. After the initial shock, the leaders began to organize the congregation and think about the future. Small groups were formed to accomplish specific tasks in the aftermath. This helped to people refocus and gave them the sense that they could do something positive to counteract the tragedy. Some members, with fire department supervision, combed the site for artifacts that could be saved. Others, because the church was a community center for many local organizations, began to find office and meeting spaces for these nonprofits hosted by the church. Another group worked on finding worship space for the congregation. And yet another group began to explore the steps required for rebuilding. Throughout the process, leaders communicated frequently with the members of the church and the organizations that had been housed there, as well as being in conversation with the neighbors and city officials about what was needed for rebuilding.

Little by little, the congregation moved away from the initial crisis and developed plans for a new building that honored their past but fit their current and future needs. People were excited and energized despite their grief at losing the old building. The innovators had lots of room for their imagination and led the way with the early adopters. They quickly persuaded the middle adopters and even many of the late adopters and laggards. A few laggards left the congregation and went elsewhere, unable to deal with the tragedy and the change, but many eventually came on board. The congregation now meets in a new building that enables them to continue their commitment to community outreach and worship. The road was not easy, but to watch sorrow and grief transformed into excitement and joy was fascinating.

Change as the Movement of the Spirit

As we have discussed throughout this chapter and in earlier chapters, change is always present in the church. It is inevitable. We cannot stop it no matter how hard we try. The question is whether we are willing to listen to the Holy Spirit in the change and prayerfully proceed to address it with sound and thoughtful strategies.

The role of the Holy Spirit is to sometimes stir up change, as we discussed in chapter 2, but the Holy Spirit is there throughout changes, with us and for us. The Spirit has given gifts—imaginative, deliberative, and questioning gifts—to every member of the congregation in order to help us grow together as community. The Spirit uses the different insights, experiences, and brokenness each of us bring to the gathered community for the building up of the body and to enable us to move through change to a strong relationship with God and each other. Together, with God surrounding us and in our midst, we help each other to become more whole and more authentically who God created us to be. God calls us into mission and that is a high calling. Such a calling often comes with a call to change that demands we rise to the occasion.

The Creator God is always creating, and that means change. Can we believe that God is in the change? Will we be faithful to God as we work with and live into the change?

Reflecting on Your Congregation . . .

1. What sorts of major change has your congregation addressed in the past ten years?

Were these changes technical, adaptive, or both?

What strategies were used to address the changes?

Do you consider the strategies successful? Why or why not?

What could you or the congregation have done differently?

2. Consider the individuals in your congregation.

Can you identify who are usually the innovators and the early adopters?

How about early majority, late majority, and laggards?

Do these people consistently play these roles, or do they shift depending on the issue?

What strategies have leaders used in the past to persuade each group?

Have these strategies been successful? If not, why not? If yes, why did they work?

3. Identify a significant change on the horizon for your congregation. How might you use the information in this chapter to begin to strategize how to successfully manage that change?

4

How Can Conflict Be Positive?

Strategies for Working with and Thriving Through Disagreement

As is probably clear by now, the inevitable changes that happen in congregations usually bring conflict. This chapter offers a more detailed explanation of conflict and strategies to address the different levels of conflict that may be present within a congregation. We will also look at conflict resolution styles and the impact that individual styles may have on managing and thriving in conflict.

How Conflict Arises

Conflict can be defined as a difference in ideas, feelings, or opinions that prevents agreement between people and groups. The degree of conflict often has to do with the reason for it as well as how quickly and effectively it is dealt with. Conflict in congregations can arise out of disagreements over moral issues, money, plans for mission, lack of growth, too much growth, pastoral style, and even for no apparent reason at all. With so many different issues that can lead to conflict, it is no wonder that addressing conflict in congregations is challenging for everyone involved, including leaders, staff, congregants, and potential new members.

Sometimes we can get to the cause for conflict, and other times there is no obvious source. Whether intentionally or unintentionally, expectedly or unexpectedly, sometimes the sermon is the source. A pastor friend of mine who was well liked by both men and women and related well to both genders preached a sermon on the emotionally charged topic of domestic violence. Typically after his sermons congregants joked with him and thanked him for his thoughtful preaching. They were generally at least friendly. But after that sermon he noticed that only some of the men spoke with him as they left the church. The women, on the other hand, hugged him and thanked him. He was never quite sure if he had inadvertently addressed abuse happening in the homes of his parishioners or if he had somehow offended the men of the congregation because, in general, he stood up for the rights of women in his sermon. He had not accused anyone in the congregation of abusing his spouse, but it became clear that some of the men felt accused or at least offended. The women seemed to be happy that someone in the church had recognized that some women felt unsafe in their own homes. He listened carefully to conversations and referred a few people to resources in the community to help address domestic violence. The tension that developed between him and some of his parishioners created a difficult period in his ministry. It took some time before relationships went back to the way they were before the sermon. He was not sorry for preaching the sermon, but he learned quickly the effect of his words on people in the pews.

I learned the same lesson about the power of words and the conflict that misunderstanding can create because I innocently teased a parishioner at a party, and she took it as an official pronouncement against her. This person and I had teased each other many times, but this day I crossed a line I was not aware of, and she took it personally. Rumors began to surface that I treated people unfairly and was not pastoral. There was never any concrete evidence offered, just generalized accusations made. Since this woman was on the council, she began to sabotage and sometimes openly challenge me on items brought before the council. It took a while for her to tell me why she was so angry with me, but we finally worked through the impasse, the negative behaviors stopped, and we could work together again.

While these two examples of conflict were generated by isolated events—a sermon and an off-hand comment—the most complicated forms of conflict in congregations are caused by systemic problems that compound the friction and create a kind of death spiral. A congregation I was involved with had reached a major breakdown, presumably over the consistent decline in giving over a few years. The decline could be attributed to a number of factors, not the least of which was that the demographics of the congregation's membership had shifted to more young families with less disposable income. Longtime members were unable to see this demographic shift, and the hunt was on to blame someone, which created further unrest, a decline in attendance and membership, and a greater drain on resources.

What had once been a flagship congregation was struggling to function fully, and the discord continued to spread. Staff members were laid off and, in the midst of an already bad situation, a beloved staff member resigned because of an extramarital affair. With the congregation reeling from that news, the situation quickly degraded even further. The shortage of staff forced the copastors to assume more administrative work, which took them away from pastoral work and worship preparation. Everything, from the quality of sermons to the pastors' availability to visit shut-ins and carry out other pastoral care work, was affected. People were upset and growing more so.

> We all have experiences and knowledge that can help us make good and wise decisions together. However, because these various points of view differ, we often perceive them to be in conflict.

Several attempts were made to assess the situation, but they too were botched. Parishioners organized a data-gathering process to identify members' concerns and hopes for the congregation. While helpful at some levels, it mostly created more disagreement over the results. Leaders brought in counselors to address the dissension through listening sessions. The counselors, however, were not particularly skilled in managing group process and so designed sessions that were long enough to let people express their views but not long enough to bring closure to the hurt raised in the sessions. People left the listening sessions more ramped up emotionally than when they came in, and this, too, exacerbated the conflict.

Finally, in response to all that was happening, a small group began to circulate a petition asking for the resignation of the copastors, which caused the congregation to break into sides for and against the resignations, even among the families of those who initiated the petition.

Ultimately, one of the copastors left voluntarily, and the other stayed for one more year to try to mend fences. A skilled interim pastor came on board and did the hard work of uncovering what had been going on and was still going on, and began to rebuild the congregation's confidence in itself. The interim also replaced some leaders and refocused the congregation on its mission and vision. By the time the new pastor was called, the congregation had moved through the conflict, learned new skills about communicating and working together, and adopted a clearer sense of its mission and vision. This last step was essential for calling a new pastor. Because the congregation knew where it wanted to go, it was able to better search for a pastor who had the skills and passions to lead them there.

Common Sources of Conflict

Conflict occurs in churches for myriad reasons, and each of these reasons, when intertwined with difficult behaviors, creates confusion and frustration that only adds to the conflict. The more complex the issue or the people involved in the conflict, the more difficult it is to sort out and manage. Often conflict in congregations is rooted in five kinds of human activities. Each can lead to conflict, and each needs to be addressed appropriately for the situation.

Different Points of View

The first source of conflict is the various points of view different people bring to a situation. This is actually a strength for congregational decision making, because we all have experiences and knowledge that can help us make good and wise decisions together. However, because these various points of view differ, we often perceive them to be in conflict. These different perspectives need not escalate tensions, but if we don't know how to manage different viewpoints well, different ways of seeing the same thing can unnecessarily turn into a fight.

Unintentional Error

The second reason for conflict is good old-fashioned human error. It is unintentional yet can lead to consequences both trivial and serious. We hope that mistakes will not be made, but sometimes they are, and we must deal with them by according individuals as much grace and as many chances to right the wrong as possible. Historically the church does not tolerate mistakes well. Examples of this kind of human failure include people volunteering to host coffee hour or serve as liturgist at worship and forgetting, or someone inadvertently leaving an article out of the bulletin or newsletter. These are minor incidents, but at times we launch a major hunt for the guilty, and resentments develop between members of a congregation.

Intentional Wrongdoing

The third source of conflict is intentional maleficence. These acts cause harm, and the agents of harm know full well what they are doing and do it anyway. Depending on the situation, these sorts of failures must be dealt with immediately and with consequences appropriate to the harm done. In the case of misconduct, if a crime was committed it must be reported to the proper authorities, both within the church and to civil authorities. A clear case here would involve the sexual abuse of children.

Selfish Actions

The fourth source of conflict arises when we put our individual needs above the needs of the congregation as a whole. It is related to intentional wrongdoing but with less evil intention. An example of selfish actions leading to human failure is a person who feels powerless in many areas of her life and who seeks out positions of power in the congregation, such as on church committees, only to wreak havoc in those positions. There are also individuals who may sense a call to ministry but for whatever reasons do not pursue that call and then act to overshadow or undermine the pastor.

Risk Taking

The final source of conflict is risk taking on behalf of the congregation. Congregations and church leaders need to take risks if we are going to fulfill the mission God calls us to. Trying new things, experimenting, and working on the cutting edge will always bring the possibility of failure, yet risk taking moves us forward as churches. We need to give people permission to experiment. Of course, we shouldn't do this without thought and consultation, but we need to keep in mind that no one will try new things if the environment is not safe.

The church is made up of fallible and finite people, but this does not negate the grace and power of God to work through us. People make mistakes. People disagree. People understand the demands of faith differently. We are each at different points on our faith journeys and may not understand the particular situation at hand from the same vantage.

Types of Conflict

Our tendency is to think that conflict is an either/or proposition. We are in conflict, or we are not. We tend to forget that even minor tensions or disagreements present a level of conflict that must be addressed, or the problems can escalate. Conflict does not have to be the result of big, scary positions taken. Ugly behavior by a single congregant counts as conflict. (Consider the bad apple that spoils the barrel.) Conflict is present at some level in almost every day of a congregation's life. The question is, What is the level, and how do we appropriately address it?

One of the foremost authorities on conflict resolution in the church is Speed Leas, who worked much of his career for the former Alban Institute. In his book *Moving Your Church Through Conflict*, Leas identifies five levels of conflict, from the lowest to the highest:

1. Problems to solve
2. Disagreement
3. Contest
4. Fight or flight
5. Intractable situations[1]

Just as we need to understand the difference between technical and adaptive change, as we discussed in chapter 3, we must identify what level of conflict is present in the congregation. The level of conflict dictates the strategy for addressing it.

Level 1: Problems to Solve

The first level of conflict, "problems to solve," is simply that—a problem that is clear and easily defined. Individuals in the congregation may disagree over how to solve the problem, but overall those engaged in decision making are able to focus on the problem and discuss solutions in a reasonable manner. As Leas explains, "At this level the parties will be problem-oriented and not person-oriented."[2] Clear-cut decisions like replacing a boiler, hiring a new church secretary, or decorating the sanctuary for Advent or Christmas are just some of the examples of conflict in this category.

Level 2: Disagreement

Level 2 conflict takes the problem in level 1 and ramps up the tension as people become invested less in the problem and more in their own interests and ideas for solutions, developing strategies to recruit people to their way of thinking. Individuals become less cooperative and less willing to exchange information, and begin to attack the other side in conversations veiled in sarcasm and humor. Yet some people are willing to listen and resolution with relatively minimal damage to relationships and the congregation as a whole is a possibility.

An example of disagreement could be a conflict that occurred in a church that for many years had had a service on Thanksgiving morning. It had been created by the former pastor's wife, and she made it go for years. When her husband retired, people tried to maintain the service, but slowly attendance began to dwindle to just a few folks. The pastor didn't lead or even attend it. Eventually, the group coming was so small that leaders had to admit there was no longer enough interest to continue the service. The few people who liked it, however, began to argue, "It is the only service this one member attends during the year." These folks then reminded leaders that that man had a lot of money that he would probably want to give to the church when he died. Leaders decided to talk with the individual, explain the situation, and encourage him to participate in other ways at the church. The man was disappointed but completely understood that the service couldn't continue with so few participants. Making the change was a struggle, but eventually members accepted it, and the church moved on.

Level 3: Contest

At the "contest" level, individuals are focused on winning. The players involved begin to lose perspective and the ability to truly listen to anything others are saying, focusing instead on steering more people to their point of view. Sides form, the rhetoric heats up, and the fight is on. There is an old saying, "Perception is reality," and this is a strong component of level 3 conflict. Whatever the perception of the situation, the solutions, and the people involved, this becomes reality for the perceiver despite evidence to the contrary, and with these perceptions, disinformation begins to rapidly spread. At this stage, the issue becomes an all-or-nothing situation. Lines are drawn between parties on either side of the issue. Unless this level of conflict is arrested at its early stages, the congregation will need outside help to de-escalate the situation and begin to move toward a conflict resolution.

Conflict escalation to level 3 is more probable when sensitive issues in which people are heavily invested are at stake, such as ethical or financial issues. I was asked to help out at a congregation at one point after the pastor was found to be plagiarizing her sermons. This congregation had always prided themselves on having outstanding preaching, and everyone was shocked when a member discovered online the same sermon he had heard the pastor preach. The pastor had used a particular phrase in the sermon, and the member decided to search for it on the Internet because it fascinated him. When he put the phrase in his search engine, not only did the phrase come up, but so did the rest of the sermon.

When confronted, the pastor admitted to plagiarizing, but the incident led to a full-scale investigation of not only her sermons, but any other complaint a member had with her. She admitted to plagiarizing about 80 percent of her sermons. She also admitted she was suffering from depression. The leaders of the congregation had a battle on their hands. Some members wanted the pastor dismissed outright, others wanted some sort of punishment delivered, and others wanted to offer compassion and help for her, because overall they thought her ministry was effective. Eventually, denominational leaders intervened and began to de-escalate the growing conflict. Despite all the rhetoric and threats of withheld giving, in the end the leaders put her on a three-month sabbatical at partial salary and encouraged her to get help for the depression. She eventually returned to her ministry, healthier and ready to engage the work before her.

Level 4: Fight or Flight

Level 4 conflict, "fight or flight," is signified by three major characteristics. First is the clear sense that those congregants invested in the issue are going to either fight to win or flee the congregation altogether. This flight is sometimes temporary (watching the fight from a distance), and sometimes it is permanent. Those not invested in the fight will either go underground or leave the congregation—temporarily or for good. Either way there is an exodus. Members' resignations from positions on committees, boards, and councils are common at this stage. Others do not resign but simply stop showing up.

Flight in one form or another will heighten the tension as people become more frustrated with the situation and the congregation becomes less able to focus on its mission and ministry. Those congregants digging in on the various sides may take on a martyr complex that only serves to make them feel more justified in their fight. The longer the situation goes on, the less we are able to have any constructive dialogue.

The second characteristic of level 4 is that the dialogue takes an ugly turn. It is no longer just about winning the argument but about punishing those on the opposite side. We begin thinking, or at least acting as if, the issue may not win on its merits, but it can perhaps win on the basis of the opponents' lack of integrity. The fight becomes intensely personal, with the opposite side deemed evil and untrustworthy, for example. People who used to worship and work together become the focus of personal attack. And those attacking become unable to see the pain and harm they are inflicting. Leas describes the players as having an "unforgiving, cold self-righteousness."[3]

> The church is made up of fallible and finite people, but this does not negate the grace and power of God to work through us.

A third characteristic of level 4 conflict in some instances is the recruitment of those outside the congregation to bolster the cause of one side or the other. These outsiders are invested in a particular side; they are not there to provide expertise or knowledge. This is often the case when the issue is an ethical one, such as abortion, equal marriage rights, or immigration. Individuals representing a particular viewpoint will seek to "help" the congregation and under that guise will try to convince people to join their side. Often these people are skilled in escalating conflict through tactics that are based in ideology and emotion rather than reason. Each faction is unwilling to listen to other points of view or compromise. Their only interest is winning through annihilation of the other and the other's perspective. The situation is painful and ugly. At this stage, the congregation must have help from outside the congregation that is neutral and skilled at conflict resolution.

The conflict may escalate to this level as the result of poor leadership in handling a situation. Take, for example, a liberal mainline Protestant church, founded in the mid-1950s in the upper Midwest. Founding members are still active in the congregation.

Several years ago, the church's leaders became aware that the pastor was having a problem with substance abuse. A few of the leaders responded: (1) support the pastor by sending him for treatment (presented to the congregation as a "sabbatical"), and (2) do not tell the congregation's members or the full leadership body what is taking place. This decision was made out of compassion for the pastor and his family and the hope that he would return from treatment in recovery, renewed in his ministry, and life would go on.

The pastor went through a bona fide treatment program and returned to the congregation and full-time ministry with the assurance that he was in recovery and handling it well. After a time, however, the same key leaders realized there was a problem. In addition, complaints were surfacing about the pastor's ministry and particularly his interpersonal skills. The pastor was not following through on his recovery program, and the leadership body, in consultation with the appropriate denominational officials, recommended that the board dismiss him from the ministry. Those officials had also been aware of the initial decision to send the pastor to treatment and not to inform others about that course of action or the problems that had surfaced due to the addiction.

The congregation erupted in anger and conflict when it learned the pastor had been fired and that he had been in a treatment program during his "sabbatical." Members of the congregation have said in retrospect they were not sure which made them angrier, the firing of the pastor or the cover-up of his problem. In either case, distrust of the leaders became rampant within the congregation, as did distrust between its leaders and the denominational leaders. The congregation broke into factions, and people began to leave the church.

A problem that was initially perceived as very serious but manageable became in a few months a full-blown conflict that threatened to destroy the congregation. When an interim pastor arrived on the scene and consulted with denominational officials, it became clear that not only did the congregation need a strong interim, but they also needed outside consultation to heal the breaches and help the congregation become fully functioning and move forward in its mission. This process took two years, but the congregation emerged stronger and healthier at the end of it.

Level 5: Intractable Situations

For this last category, Leas offers this description: "Level 5 conflicts are not within the control of the participants; they are conflict run amok."[4] No one can see clearly. The objective at this level is to destroy your opponent, even if it means destroying the congregation in the process. The rhetoric becomes more ideological, without any logical reasoning or ability to listen to other points of view. The sides see themselves engaged in a great battle. As Leas describes the conflict, they are "part of an eternal cause, fighting for universal principles."[5] Each side believes God is on their side, which makes it harder to stop fighting. Indeed, we somehow come to a place where we are thinking only about how the fighting will continue. Most members who are reasonable and have a healthy perspective leave the congregation. And those left only have one option: fight or seek outside help.

Those who still care deeply about the congregation will struggle in the midst of the fighting, and at this level the only recourse is outside intervention. I worked with one congregation where the members were suing each other in the midst of a disagreement about the handling of a case of clergy sexual misconduct. The interim pastor and I worked to try to lower the conflict level and get people sitting down to talk with one another. It was a long and difficult battle. No one walked away unscathed and the congregation had to set upon a course of rebuilding itself when the conflict finally ended with several key players, including the clergyperson in question, agreeing to leave the congregation.

Denial Is Not a Solution

Leas's five-stage continuum of conflict applies in cases where people at least acknowledge that they have a problem to be solved. Many congregations are not yet on the continuum, as they are still in denial that there is conflict at all. The longer denial functions in a congregation, the greater the subterranean damage. Emotions escalate, and misinformation spreads. Factions form, even if they are not acknowledged, and fights usually start erupting about nonsensical matters while the real source of conflict simmers just below the surface. Twelve Step programs have a saying, "You are only as sick as your secrets," and this certainly applies to congregations. When members mutually conspire not to acknowledge problems or actively pretend they do not exist, healing and solutions are impossible. Conflict needs light and air to have a chance at resolution.

I once interviewed for an interim position at a congregation whose former pastor was known to have been sexually inappropriate with adult members of the congregation and in the wider community. That behavior was a primary factor in the congregation's leaders asking him to resign.

> When members mutually conspire not to acknowledge problems or actively pretend they do not exist, healing and solutions are impossible. Conflict needs light and air to have a chance at resolution.

During my interview I asked what approaches had been discussed to help the congregation heal from this situation. The search committee responded that they did not know what I was talking about. There was no problem to be addressed in the congregation, and they even acted as if I had offended them. Their response enabled me to quickly eliminate them from consideration in my own job search. Over time the effects of the former pastor's misconduct played out in the congregation in a multitude of ways, and it has taken many years for the congregation to get on its feet again. It is still a shadow of its former self, but it is finally moving in the right direction.

Getting people to admit there is a problem is a difficult task, especially if they are in real denial. Sometimes it is not possible and then we have to decide whether we can work within a situation of denial or if we must begin to consider other options for a place of ministry or church membership. Before deciding to leave, however, we can try to present evidence of the problem and hope to persuade others to see the reality before us. Or we can ask people to consider what their hopes are for the congregation and what might be keeping those things from happening. With this latter strategy, the hope is that people will see the disconnect between their desires and the reality and that will open the door to discuss the problem.

Leadership in Times of Conflict

Leaders need to facilitate conflict-resolving conversation in an atmosphere of prayer and discernment. Congregations are not like corporations, where the bottom line is the primary focus. Congregations must be good stewards of our dollars, but they must also be faithful stewards of our other resources and particularly of the mission God has given us. God's call to mission sometimes requires risk taking and almost always pushes us out of our comfort zones. That alone can be anxiety producing. The leaders' task is to help people through that anxiety and inspire them to respond faithfully and take risks to carry out God's call.

These responsibilities imply at least two things for leaders. First, we must learn to manage our own stress and anxiety. The second implication is that as leaders, we must consciously and actively seek to grow in our skills and capacities to facilitate discernment, conflict management, and change.

Being a Nonanxious Presence

Being a nonanxious presence begins with understanding what might cause us anxiety. Just as we must identify the level of the conflict, we need to know how we generally prefer to deal with conflict. Think about your conflict management style. Are you a conflict avoider? Do you need to study the situation and gather more information before you are comfortable moving forward? Do you tend to lose perspective and turn the proverbial molehill into a mountain? Do you actually enjoy conflict and, in fact, tend to stir it up if things get too complacent? Being aware of your personal style and using that information as part of the process of dealing with conflict is key to successfully managing conflict.

If you know your style is to avoid conflict, it will be important to work with other leaders who are comfortable dealing with conflict and can help to work through it. If you understand your style to be more aggressive in dealing with conflict, it may be helpful to have others who can temper the conflict management style to one that helps people hear and respond to the leaders rather than being put off by an in-your-face sort of manner.

Whatever your style, effective leadership in times of conflict depends on offering a nonanxious presence. This means even if you are internally tied in knots over an issue, you do not project your anxiety onto others, including the congregation.

The impact of leaders' anxiety was obvious in a conversation I was invited to lead at a small, fairly conservative congregation in the upper Midwest. Two or three people had written to the church council stating they wanted to have a conversation as a congregation about becoming welcoming to LGBTQ people. The pastor, while supportive of this idea, was terrified of the potential conflict and suggested they bring someone in who could facilitate a group inquiry about whether to have the conversation. I was that facilitator.

About twenty people stayed after worship one Sunday to participate in the inquiry. We sat in a circle in the church basement and began to have a conversation. No one seemed adamantly opposed to LGBTQ people, but some congregants did not want to proclaim publicly that LGBTQ people were welcome at the church. Others wanted to do so as a witness of hospitality and inclusion to their small and fairly conservative town, one where LGBTQ people were not particularly welcome. Back and forth the conversation went about what such a statement would mean and, if they were to go about making such a proclamation, how they would do so.

What became apparent was that the pastor's anxiety was influencing the group. The group's anxiety was particularly high when the conversation started. People seemed hesitant to talk, and when they did, their voices were loud and tense. The pastor tried to manage her anxiety, but her body language spoke volumes. She looked tense, and she hunched over in a way that was closed, as if she were protecting herself. She laughed nervously and at inappropriate times. Overall, the message was, *I am frightened of what will happen and just want to get this over with.*

As I moved the group into conversation and modeled a calm and nonanxious presence, everyone, including the pastor, began to relax. I made it clear, without saying anything directly, that this was not a scary conversation. It was important, but it was not a conversation to be afraid of. No decisions needed to be made at this time. Everyone's opinion was valued, as long as the opinion was offered in a respectful way. We were just talking about the welcoming issue like any other conversation that the congregation might have had on any other given day.

The key takeaway here is this: when leaders act like a conversation or a decision is scary, it will become scary or more frightening, because people respond to the anxiety leaders demonstrate. The impact of our anxiety is even more significant if anxiety is already present in the system. So, for example, if a congregation is nervous about its future—particularly whether it has one—any issue, big or small, can create more anxiety and its accompanying symptoms and behaviors.

The job of leaders is to manage our own anxiety and the anxiety present in the congregational system. This job is not one leaders, pastoral or lay, can delegate. People will interpret reticence, abdication, or anxiety as a clue that they have reason to become more anxious. Leaders have the job of lowering anxiety, not ramping it up. Lowering anxiety is not the same as placating, however. Lowering anxiety is about helping people feel calm, which allows for passionate but reasoned dialogue. Still, we need to perform a balancing act to maintain enough tension so people are motivated to address the issue at hand yet dissipate tension to the point people are able to address the issue in a reasonable, articulate manner.

What Is Your Conflict Management Style?

Being aware of your personal style and using that information as part of the process of dealing with conflict is key to successfully managing conflict. Think about your style:

- Are you a conflict avoider?

- Do you need to study the situation and gather more information before you are comfortable moving forward?

- Do you tend to lose perspective and turn the proverbial molehill into a mountain?

- Do you actually enjoy conflict and, in fact, tend to stir it up if things get too complacent?

Encouraging Self-Care and Growth

We must be careful to maintain our own emotional health and vitality in the midst of turmoil. All of us, clergy or lay, can find ourselves overcommitted and struggling to handle multiple personal situations in addition to our congregational leadership responsibilities. Finding balance, drawing boundaries, even letting go of some responsibilities through delegation or even resigning from a particular position will be crucial to maintaining personal health and well-being. Lay leaders often hold more than one leadership role in a church, particularly in a small congregation. While stepping up is admirable, to do so at the risk of one's health and emotional well-being is not helpful to the individual or the congregation. Congregations that are burning out leaders may need to seriously consider prioritizing and letting go of some activities and ministries if the current efforts of the church are demanding more than volunteer leaders can handle.

Self-care for pastors can be a difficult path as well. Pastors often find their jobs to be lonely and can become so buried in work that they frequently fail to take good care of themselves. They neglect to seek out support through spiritual direction, peer support groups, psychotherapy, or coaching; to participate in healthy recreation outside the congregation; or to pursue other avenues to health and vitality. This spells doom for a ministry, but it also means the pastor is less able to respond when conflict arises. Self-care is essential if a pastor wishes to serve in ministry for the long haul. Self-care can include the strategies just listed, but it is also about getting exercise, maintaining a healthy diet, and nurturing a strong family life and relationships with friends outside the congregation. It also means drawing good boundaries by taking days off and going on vacation, as well as not allowing congregants to demand attention 24/7.

By taking care of ourselves, we model for others in the congregation the value of self-care. If all congregational leaders are committed to practicing good self-care and managing stress in our lives, these actions will increase our ability to manage conflict in a healthy and productive way.

Pastors and church councils should ensure education and training opportunities for leaders, whether that means funding continuing education for pastors or leadership development training for lay leaders. While some people come to leadership with good skills, we can all sharpen our skills and gain new ones.

Pastors who have the background and knowledge can provide some of this education. For example, they can train lay leaders to run effective meetings or to practice prayer and discernment in their leadership. Many denominational midlevel judicatories, such as conferences or synods, will provide training on topics such as vital church growth, stewardship, conflict management, and other important topics. Congregations can also band together with several nearby congregations and jointly sponsor training in a wide variety of topics. Another option that is increasingly available is online education through webinars and other courses.

> Leaders must be careful to maintain our own emotional health and vitality in the midst of turmoil. By taking care of ourselves, we model for others in the congregation the value of self-care.

Often I hear defeatist attitudes in congregations, expressed in comments such as "We do not have good leaders or the right kind of leaders" or "We do not have resources to send our leaders to conferences or workshops." If we believe that God is calling us to do God's work and we are willing to be creative, we can train leaders without big budgets.

Strategies for Strengthening Communities of Faith in Conflict

As discussed in earlier chapters, the goal of strengthening ourselves as communities of faith is not achieved by setting out to make everyone happy but by managing conflict while remaining faithful to the mission God is calling us to in the world. These strategies are:

1. Seeing God at work in the world and believing that God is at work in us
2. A strong understanding and practice of prayer
3. Practicing discernment to clarify our identity as a congregation and God's call to us

Each of these strategies enables us to move toward being a more faithful congregation fulfilling God's mission for us.

Seeing God at Work

First, we need to understand how God is working among us. Our understanding will depend on our theology. I come out of a progressive tradition that tends to downplay the notion that God is a significant agent in our day and age. We tend to think God gives us wisdom, but it is up to us to do the work. And I always push back on that a bit.

If, indeed, we believe God has called us together as communities of faith and that we are engaged in a mission from God, do we also believe that God would send us out to accomplish this hard, sometimes controversial work without acting on our behalf? This seems illogical to me. I argue that God is an active agent among us, and our job is to discern how God is acting with us, for us, and—sometimes—in spite of us. In conflict, the more clearly we can see God's action in our midst and God's call to us, the easier it is to move through conflict knowing that God is in it with us.

Understanding and Practicing Prayer

The second aspect of this strategy is our understanding and practice of prayer itself. What do we mean by prayer? Is prayer a perfunctory "God bless our meeting" before we dive into the work ourselves? How do we engage prayer in our conflict management? Are we willing to sit still with one another and listen together to how the Spirit might be moving? Perhaps we sit with a passage of Scripture, meditate on it, share what we heard, and then consider what this means for the conflict at hand. No matter the method of prayer, the act of making ourselves vulnerable and humble before God shifts our perspectives, especially in conflict, and opens us to new possibilities for working through and resolving the conflict that is present.

The story in chapter 2 about the congregation that thought "Happy + Nice = Church" was a situation where learning to step out of the immediate problem-solving mode and move into discernment and prayer. This shift was key for the congregation to get itself righted and refocused on mission. In that case, we spent a great deal of time with the Christ hymns in Philippians 1:27 and 2:5–11. The first time I met with the steering group in the congregation, I invited them to read and reflect on it. Everyone read it through, put it aside, and looked at me like, "Now can we get to the problem at hand?" I gently asked them to look again at the passage, and we read it for a second time. I asked all of them to consider where they got stuck or had a question as they read the passage and to share that word or phrase with the group. I made some comments about the significance of the passage and its interpretation as discussed in chapter 2. We shared a bit more and closed with prayer. Then we moved on to address conflict and congregation revitalization.

The next time we met I pulled out the Philippians passage again. I sensed some restlessness and saw a few looks that suggested, "We already read this." I asked the group to indulge me, and because they were paying me as a consultant, they did. This time people were surprised that the text had new things to say to them. We shared, prayed, and then moved on to the rest of our agenda. Each meeting the group more easily engaged with Philippians, and each meeting their sharing got deeper. They reached a point where they would gather for meetings and pull out Philippians with no prompting from me. When we began to design the congregational meeting to share the results of our work, the group wanted to begin the meeting with everyone talking in small groups about Philippians. At the meeting, I did a brief exegesis, and then the sharing took off from there. It was a powerful experience for a congregation that had not included God in its definition of church. It was a watershed moment as they began to move out of conflict and learn new ways of being together.[6]

> No matter the method of prayer, the act of making ourselves vulnerable and humble before God shifts our perspectives, especially in conflict, and opens us to new possibilities for working through and resolving the conflict that is present.

Patiently Discerning Our Identity and Calling

The third aspect of this strategy is discernment. Discernment is an ancient practice in the church but a largely forgotten one in many Christian communities. We want things to happen right now. We want reasons, explanations, and enough ambiguity to make us feel we have options. We want to purchase a fix for our problems—now. Yet our tradition teaches us that we must learn to listen, slow down, and sometimes act on intuition. Christian discernment in many ways is extremely countercultural. It demands patience and a willingness to live in the unknown, an experience most of us are at best reluctant to tolerate. It is definitely not something we do naturally.

Discernment, however, is a crucial part of decision making and managing conflict. We have to slow down and learn to listen to one another and the Holy Spirit. This is difficult when emotions are running high, and churches in severe conflict (3.5 or higher on Leas's scale) must first de-escalate the conflict and learn new ways of being together. In that process, congregations can begin to learn what this ancient practice of discernment is all about and put it into practice.

In her book *Decision Making and Spiritual Discernment: The Sacred Art of Finding Your Way*, psychologist and spiritual director Nancy L. Bieber points out that discernment involves three themes: willingness, attentiveness, and responsiveness.[7] These themes or strands are woven together, according to Bieber, in wise decision making. Practicing these strands takes time and intention. Most of the time in congregations, we are in a hurry to get the decision made and move on to the next thing. We often feel uncomfortable with slowing down and sitting with a discernment process. Sitting still and waiting is hard for many of us as individuals, and it becomes even more difficult in a congregational setting because we are asking *multiple* individuals to be still and wait. The theme of willingness reminds us that discernment requires patience and looking and listening carefully for the Spirit's presence and guidance. Bieber advises that we need to consider whether we are open to the leading of the Spirit in the first place or if we really just want to do this ourselves and leave God out of the matter. The theme of attentiveness reminds us that in our looking and listening we "consider who we are, who we dream of being, and the life situations in which we find ourselves."[8]

> Discernment is a crucial part of decision making and managing conflict. We have to slow down and learn to listen to one another and the Holy Spirit.

Often congregation members assume we know what church is about and who we are. I have done an exercise with the governing bodies of congregations in which I ask them to write down the mission or vision statement of the church—without looking it up. The answers are telling. Some admit there is no mission or vision statement. If there is one, a variety of versions of it (usually not at all close to the actual statement) are put forth by the participants. If our leaders cannot identify the congregation's statement of purpose, then how are the people in the pews going to do so? And how do we make good decisions without a clear understanding of who we are?

The final strand of discernment is responsiveness. This aspect of the discernment practice is about actually making a decision in response to what we have discovered in the process of being willing and attentive. God has opened our eyes to see and hear who we are and what the situation is so that we can then make a wise and faithful choice. Such a choice opens us up further to rely on the Spirit's leading and to grow as a congregation in faith and in faithfulness. This approach is different from the way most congregations and their governing bodies make decisions.

> In the process of slowing down, reflecting on a text, and talking about its meaning for us as a group, we begin to discover who we are and who we want to be with one another.

One of the reasons I ask groups, including entire congregations, to meditate on the Christ hymn in Philippians is that it forces them to slow down. Other texts can be used, depending on the issue at hand, but the Christ hymn offers a way to reframe conflict within the larger narrative of Christ and his redemptive work. In the process of slowing down, reflecting on the text, and talking about its meaning for us as a group, we begin to discover who we are and who we want to be with one another. This provides us with a positive experience as we learn how to have conversation, be reflective, be open to the Spirit's leading, and then consider the issue before us and its many facets. In so doing, we learn a whole new way of being church together, debating the issues respectfully and coming to a decision that feels not only right, but faithful to the calling of God.

Fostering Healthy Communications

Another strategy we must use in addressing conflict is learning how to communicate well. We are all painfully aware that meaningful conversation, effective communication, and respectful public discourse are rare in our day. Technology allows us to communicate more quickly than in any time in the history of humankind. News travels around the world faster than we can keep up with it. Being able to communicate across the globe in such amazing ways is exciting. The possibilities for communicating, gathering information, and building community are endless.

Yet even as we enjoy this blessing of communication-enhancing technology, we have learned some ugly behaviors. We are incessantly flooded by the 24/7 news cycle. We tune out much of what we are hearing, because we have information overload. We are bombarded with marketing schemes to sell us things. We are assailed by opinions from bloggers, commentators, and others who may or may not have a sound basis for the opinions they put forth, and we're often too lazy, apathetic, overwhelmed, or just plain busy to do the research to find out. We distrust the communications we receive because we are sure the communicators just want to draw us into their camp. We speak in sound bites and hashtags. We have lost the art of real conversation in the midst of so much communication.

Deep and meaningful sacred conversations are really what many of us long for, and yet they rarely take place in our congregations, because we get caught up in the day-to-day details of running the congregation or participating in endless activities.

Back in the congregation, we have a strange relationship to all of this technology and the accompanying communication styles. On the one hand, we do not participate in some aspects of communication technology. Many congregations are woefully behind on learning how to effectively use the Internet as a means of communicating and evangelizing. On the other hand, we are in some ways full participants in this aspect of our culture. We bring some of the worst sides of the communications boom to the congregation. People offer opinions without any grounding in fact, arguing on a purely emotional basis. In fact, we commonly present sound bites and opinions as facts in congregational discussions. Some church members regularly tune out others or listen to only parts of messages. We often listen to another person just long enough to hear a bit of what she is saying and then start arguing back. And we use forceful rhetoric to keep our fears and each other at a distance. True conversation and dialogue are a lost art in many congregations. We need to learn all over again.

> To truly discover who we are as a congregation and to understand not only our identity, but also the mission and vision we are called to by God, we must learn to have conversations that lead us into deeper relationship with one another and with God.

Diane M. Millis, founder of the Journey Conversations Project, offers helpful suggestions in her book *Conversation— The Sacred Art: Practicing Presence in an Age of Distraction*, for fostering deep and meaningful sacred conversations. Such conversations are really what many of us long for, and yet they rarely take place in our congregations. We get caught up in the day-to-day details of running the congregation or participating in endless activities and we fail to take the time to really listen to one another. Millis describes the challenges we face:

> A good conversation, like a good meal, is something we continue to savor over time. For those of us who live in the twenty-first century's digitalized world, we feel as if we have far less time to savor much, whether food, relationships, or conversations. Many of us find that in our effort to maintain a breadth of connection, we compromise the depth of our connections. We often feel distracted, as we struggle to keep up with all the messages that fill our screens, unable to bring our full attention to any single encounter, let alone have ample time to reflect on them.[9]

Guidelines for Healthy Communication

Everyone's input is equally important.

Each of us is an expert on our own experience. We all have valuable information to share.

We encourage attentive listening from everyone involved.

Our goal for the conversation is to learn and expand our understanding. We reach that goal through careful listening.

We ask that everyone participates and that no one dominates.

Actively verbal participants are encouraged to monitor the frequency and length of their contributions. All of us work to create an atmosphere of trust, so quieter participants feel safe chiming in.

When giving feedback, we stick to describing behavior.

We avoid adding evaluative comments that may overstep boundaries with our own editorializing. Judgmental language such as "should" and "ought" is discouraged.

We encourage people to tell their own stories and speak of their own experiences . . .

. . . and avoid representing the grievances of others.

We encourage collaborative dialogue.

We do not try to outdo one another by showing how much we know about the topic we are discussing. We don't engage in dialogue with the motive of proving others wrong. Instead, we strive to open ourselves to the views of others, so we might enlarge our understanding of multiple perspectives.

We respect and honor the confidentiality of all private information.

While we encourage people to own their feedback by voicing it directly and respectfully to the concerned party, we recognize that in the context of our conversations, sensitive or confidential information may be shared. When this occurs, we will ask permission before sharing that information with others.[10]

To truly discover who we are as a congregation and to understand not only our identity, but also the mission and vision we are called to by God, we must learn to have conversations that lead us into deeper relationship with one another and with God. This requires us to open ourselves in vulnerability and to tell our stories to one another.

Creating healthy guidelines for communication and a process for communicating in meetings and other small group settings is one of the most helpful tools for de-escalating congregational emotions (particularly anger) and relearning how to talk with one another. Once in place, these guidelines provide a structure for the conversation that everyone knows. With the boundaries established, everyone—not just the person leading the meeting—can help enforce them.

I was involved with a congregation where a team of members created communication guidelines and published them far and wide in the congregation. Many members were greatly relieved, because the guidelines helped end the domination and bullying by a few members in their congregational meetings and smaller gatherings. Large wall posters of the guidelines were prepared and hung in the fellowship hall. Copies of the guidelines were placed on each table in meeting rooms, so everyone could refer to them. Near the beginning of a congregational meeting, the president would ask a member of the team that drafted the guidelines to read them aloud to remind everyone what they said.

The leaders appointed a chaplain—someone other than the pastor—to serve as the spiritual guide for every meeting. If conversation got overly heated, the chaplain had the authority to call for a time of silence and prayer. The effect was to re-center everyone, calm things down, and let people catch a deep breath before continuing in conversation. The chaplain also offered prayer at the beginning, before a vote, and at the end of the meeting. The person chosen was a longtime lay leader with a gift for prayer who was well respected by everyone in the congregation. Meetings began to change dramatically with the use of the guidelines and the chaplain.

The first few times the guidelines were used, leaders offered a short training session and explanation. After that they were simply read, distributed, and posted on the walls. Before long people began to police themselves and, on rare occasion, each other. In addition, comments were limited to two minutes per person, and a person could not speak to an issue a second time until everyone who wanted to speak had done so.

Some people were unhappy with the decision to use the guidelines and to limit the amount of time and number of times people could speak, but as the congregation became more skilled in conversing and working together, even the recalcitrant few began to come around. Learning to practice healthy communication was not easy, but it was well worth the effort. The congregation is growing and thriving and has developed many new and exciting ministries to the wider community and even the global church.

Strategies for Each Level of the Continuum

Each level of conflict offers challenges, and while some strategies can be used in all levels, some strategies are more appropriate in addressing conflict at specific levels of Leas's continuum. The one strategy that needs to be a part of every conversation is prayer and discernment. The more people are reminded of where they are, who they are, and to whom they belong, the more the conversation can remain focused on discerning how the congregation can be faithful to God's calling.

Conflicts at level 1 are managed with good leadership. If a congregation has good conversation habits, addressing an issue at this level should be fairly simple. The guidelines help, of course. The biggest challenge is not to make a mountain out of a molehill. Sometimes in hopes of taking an issue seriously, leaders will inadvertently escalate the emotions around an issue. The calmer and less anxious leaders can be while still taking an issue seriously, the better.

Conflict management at level 2 is greatly enhanced by using the guidelines to facilitate the conversation and deal with potential emotions. Leaders should ensure that no one dominates. Leaders need to also encourage folks to speak up if they are not doing so. Simply asking people to go around a circle and state their opinion can do a great deal to get the conversation rolling. Be sure to find ways for all participants to speak. Sometimes people wait to hear what those who traditionally dominate conversations have to say and then imitate them. Inviting a balance in voices between the dominant and the less dominant may completely shift the conversation. To create a balance and to allow those who are more introverted an opportunity to think through comments they may wish to make, it is helpful to offer a bit of reflection time before anyone speaks. Such a reflection time may allow the less dominant members of the group to be more comfortable speaking. A reflection time may frustrate those who like to dominate, but that is part of growing together in community.

Level 3 conflict demands even clearer and more formal procedures for conversation. Here making the guidelines visible, having them read, and making use of a chaplain are probably wise. At this level, emotions begin to ramp up, and the tensions begin to seriously escalate. The initial goal at this level is to de-escalate emotions and get people refocused on the issue, common goals in solving the issue, and the mission of the congregation. By doing those things, leaders enable calmer, more focused conversation.

Once the conflict passes the halfway point of level 3 and people are focusing on each other and their positions, managing the conflict without some sort of outside intervention is virtually impossible. At this halfway point—and after it—skilled intervention is helpful. This could be provided by a well-respected pastor or lay leader from a neighboring congregation or by a denominational leader. The person should be from outside the congregation, have no vested interest in the matter at hand, and have the skills to facilitate a prayerful process of conversation.

> Sometimes in hopes of taking an issue seriously, leaders will inadvertently escalate the emotions around an issue. The calmer and less anxious leaders can be while still taking an issue seriously, the better.

Sadly, if the conflict continues to escalate to level 4 or 5, the congregation most likely will have to bring in a consultant with specific skills in conflict resolution and mediation. Congregations are reluctant to invest the money required in such cases, but we need to recognize that an investment at this stage could save the congregation's life. If the choice is between allowing continued conflict to destroy the congregation or making an investment in a consultant to help manage, resolve, and move beyond the conflict, then the cost of a consultant looks more acceptable. Congregations that do not engage consultants at levels 4 and 5 are usually destined to see more destruction and even closure of the congregation.

Reflecting on Your Congregation . . .

1. Consider one or two major conflicts in your congregation's past.

   What level of conflict did they reach?

   How were they managed?

   Who were the major players?

   What was the outcome?

   What can you learn from what happened?

2. What has been the role of prayer and discernment in your approach to conflict?

3. How does your congregation have conversations?

   Do you have guidelines or a process for congregational conversation?

   If so, are they effective? How might you strengthen them?

   If you don't have guidelines, what are some rules you would find helpful?

4. Choose a potential conflict that is likely in your congregation in the near future. Create a strategy for addressing it based on the material in this chapter.

   What strategies will be the easiest to implement?

   What will be the most difficult?

5

Why Do We Love Extremes?

Developing Imagination and Managing Polarities

Congregations must make choices if we want to change, grow, and adapt to the changing world around us and the changing circumstances in our own lives. Yet many congregations think and act as if we do not have choices. Or we frame the options in either/or terms, paying attention only to the extremes of what is actually a continuum of possibilities. This either/or approach is often based on the fear that our only alternative to the current course of action is something so dramatic—such as the death of the congregation—that we can't conceive of pursuing it. This dualistic perspective is usually a false one that exacerbates the problems many congregations face when in conflict or undergoing significant changes.

Most situations, however, offer a broad range of possibilities—if a congregation is able to entertain alternatives other than the status quo or death. Indeed, such either/or thinking usually becomes a self-fulfilling prophecy. Certainly those two extremes are possibilities, but they are not the foregone conclusions that many congregations treat them as.

Conflict and the Either/Or Trap

In my experience as a consultant, the natural default of most congregations is to take an either/or posture when assessing conflict. Debates about how to interpret the Bible provide a good example. In these conflicts, the views are often summarized as, *Conservatives take the Bible seriously and liberals do not*. This is not true—and it is not even the real issue. It is a false duality that simply confuses the conversation and keeps us from understanding each other's true positions. The reality is both sides take the Bible seriously but in different ways. There are not just two ways but a multitude of ways to interpret the Bible. Acknowledging even that much gets us out of the limiting either/or thinking and allows us to broaden our perspective.

Conflict narrows our ability to see possibilities, not just because we have a natural tendency to think dualistically, but because as conflict deepens, it triggers a basic and even primal reaction in our brains. We become afraid, and the fight-or-flight instinct kicks in when conflict gets severe. We are hardwired to want to fight or flee when we are afraid. Fear is a powerful motivator for all sorts of behaviors. But long before that level of conflict is reached, the ability to be creative, imaginative, and thoughtful slowly disappears and we are unable to see choices. Sides are drawn around one position or another, and finding a third, fourth, or fifth way out is next to impossible without outside intervention. As the conflict progresses, our desire to fight with each other increases, as well as the instinct to leave the congregation altogether. At a time when the congregation needs people to be most imaginative, we become the least imaginative.

Conflict often robs congregations of the desire to even entertain choices. Once we become locked in an either/or duality, we don't want to see other possibilities. This recalcitrance only leads to more bad behavior and a denial of the ability of God to work in our midst. And if God is locked out of our conversations because we refuse to see anything other than our point of view, we are denying the very source of our calling as a congregation to enter in and be a part of us. We cease to be church.

Imagination as God's Gift

Our gift of imagination is a birthright. God endowed us with creative, imaginative capacities from the very beginning of time. The Hebrew Scriptures begin with the creation of the world, and at the heart of that story is God's proclamation that we are made in the divine image.

> Then God said, "Let us make humankind in our image, according to our likeness; and let them have dominion over the fish of the sea, and over the birds of the air, and over the cattle, and over all the wild animals of the earth, and over every creeping thing that creeps upon the earth." So God created humankind in his image, in the image of God he created them; male and female he created them. (Genesis 1:26–27)

At the heart of the divine image is the creative spark, imagination. The root of "imagination" and "image" is the same, *imago*. While the Latin translates this root as "image," the word has been imbued with many meanings over the centuries in Christian theology. If we are truly made in the image of God, then we carry in our human DNA the attributes of the Divine, including the ability to imagine and create. We are not the Creator, but we do share in cocreation through the use of our imagination and intellect. We were given these gifts to share the work of our Creator in the world. And what good is a gift if it is never used?

Lack of Imagination in the Church

If we are the bearers of these gifts, we must ask the question, Why don't we use them in the church? We can be exceptionally creative outside of the church. People often accomplish amazing things in their work and personal lives. Yet we often seem to leave our imagination and creativity at the door when we arrive at church. We are stuck in a rut—*This is how we do church*—and we cannot imagine anything different. We follow organizational patterns that served the church well at the time they were created but that no longer serve our needs. Small congregations are top-heavy and use cumbersome structure and governance they do not need. We repeat the same programming year after year with little variation. And we return to the familiar when seeking solutions to problems, even if the familiar no longer applies. We neglect the gifts of creativity and imagination that are our

> Conflict narrows our ability to see possibilities. At a time when the congregation needs people to be most imaginative, we become the least imaginative.

birthright. We deny the very assets that demonstrate we are made in the image of God.

I spent a year studying churches that meet on the Internet. With one exception these churches do not meet face-to-face. The one exception includes both a face-to-face community and a large online following. One of the arenas for my study was an online world called Second Life. In Second Life people may create a whole new world. Participants might choose an avatar of any gender or even a non-human to represent themselves, build houses, develop alternative careers, or create worshipping communities. Second Life offers people an opportunity to create a world for themselves online.

> We can be exceptionally creative in our lives outside of church. Yet we often seem to leave our imagination and creativity at the door when we arrive at church.

Second Life includes a large number of faith communities, and with a couple of exceptions, each has more or less replicated church as we currently know it. I expected to find a great deal of creativity and imagination exercised, given the freedom people had to create church. After all, no one is beholden to denominational or ecclesiastical authorities in Second Life. Yet apparently people could not conceive of anything different from what they knew. Instead of taking advantage of that freedom, churches in Second Life were essentially re-creations of churches we already know. The buildings look the same. The liturgy is the same—sometimes even more stilted and awkward than worship in the traditional and face-to-face world.

If churches online are unable to create something new and different, we should not be surprised that churches in the traditional world struggle to do things in new and different ways.

Reclaiming the Richness of Faith

In addition to finding ways to spark our imaginations, we also need to reclaim the rich faith we have. Christian faith is filled with a depth of meaning. We seem, however, to reach for simplistic and even trite meaning, and in a sense we flatten what could be rich and deep in expression into a one-dimensional faith. Our faith sounds more like a greeting card at times than the wide range of expression we find in the Bible. Of course, simplistic faith is sometimes a tactic for minimizing conflict. If we stay on the surface, we won't offend anyone or stir anything up. Then simplifying becomes a habit that robs us of our ability to access a deeper theology. My observation crosses many different denominational and theological lines.

More liberal churches are so afraid of not following the latest scholarship in biblical studies that they rob the biblical text of its vitality, and preaching becomes an academic exercise. Or churches are so heavily engaged in social justice work that they lose sight of the reasons they do that work in the first place. The work becomes divorced from the Spirit of God moving among them, and the power of that connection is lost.

Conservative churches flatten faith by reducing it to a series of moral propositions that lock in "God's position" on matters of life and faith. Or they focus on saving souls to the exclusion of teaching those souls what it means to grow in faith. The joy of a life of faith is lost in the flurry of saving people from eternal damnation and an immoral lifestyle.

Both sides have missed the heart of the Gospel message and the purpose of church. And our secular culture continues to grow more distant and less interested in what is happening on Sunday morning or other days of the week. The church leaders and members seem to lack a real understanding of the lives and struggles of ordinary people outside of the church, and the church appears more a museum to an era gone by.

Reclaiming the richness of our faith by engaging more deeply in spiritual practices such as prayer, scripture study, and mission will be helpful in reaching people who do not think we speak to their lives. Our faith is about relationships and how to live with one another. Our faith is deeply steeped in love and connections with God and each other. Our faith is intimately wrapped up in how we make a better world and create meaningful and abundant lives. When we tap that richness and depth, we will find a way to connect with those who think we have nothing to say to them or the world.

Congregational Life Cycle and Imagination

Being imaginative and reclaiming our rich faith are two ways to affect the creative process and bring life to our congregations. Congregations are also affected by where we are in the congregational life cycle. Congregations in later stages of the life cycle have less ability to imagine and create. They can discover how to be imaginative and creative, but it takes very intentional work to do so. Let us examine the life cycle to understand better how the various stages affect our ability to change.

Just as individuals have a life cycle—we are born, mature, age, and eventually die, so congregations follow the same cycle unless an infusion of imagination and creativity at key points changes the trajectory of the journey.

Church Life Cycle

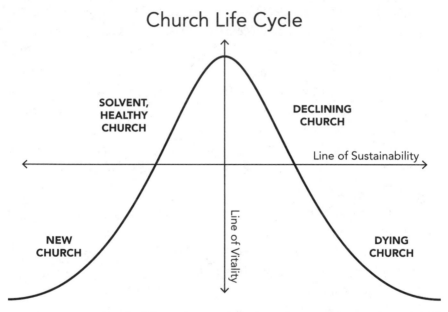

A congregation's life cycle can be viewed as a four-sectioned bell curve.[1] On the left side of the curve is the new church start, in quadrant one. New church starts are full of creativity, imagination, and hopeful anticipation about the church's potential. Members feel excitement and have a dream. The dream is not yet sustainable for the organization, but it fuels the organization into being. The congregation needs a lot of support at this stage of development.

As the dream develops and people are attracted to the ideas driving it, relationships begin to form. They will become the heart of a community of faith as it moves beyond a dream and forms a sustainable organization. It develops programs, and people are engaged and excited. This stage is the second quadrant of the life cycle. At this point, the congregation is healthy and functional, moving toward the pinnacle of the curve.

Eventually, the demands of growth and programs require that the congregation put more energy into organization and management. This is both the pinnacle of the congregation's life cycle and the danger point. If a congregation at this point does not create new and imaginative ways to engage people, it will plateau and begin to lose its ability to dream and imagine new possibilities. As dreams die, the church begins to experience decline and moves into the third quadrant. The third quadrant is where leadership gives way to management, putting more emphasis on policies and procedures, reporting and control. Creativity and new ideas are no longer encouraged. The goal is maintaining the status quo.

> When leadership gives way to management, putting more emphasis on policies and procedures, reporting and control, then creativity and new ideas are no longer encouraged.

Very few new people are attracted to the congregation at this point, and some who have been engaged move away or become less active due to their own aging or waning lack of interest. As people begin to disengage, the relationships that were forged around the earlier dreams begin to fade, and sustaining programming and congregational vitality becomes harder. The congregation will usually experience rapid decline to the point where it can barely maintain a pastor or even worship. With this rapid decline congregations move into the fourth quadrant in the life cycle and are no longer able to sustain themselves. Eventually, without significant intervention and re-invention of itself, the congregation will die.

While this a normal cycle, it is not an inevitable one. Congregations can and do reinvent themselves using the gifts of imagination and creativity as they listen to God's call and discern new directions. Such reinvention requires a lot of work and a willingness to let go of the old in order to make way for the new. This work can be fraught with conflict as the congregation goes through major changes. Congregations that learn to catch themselves at the beginning of plateaus will find making changes a bit easier, but nevertheless it isn't without effort and some tension. Congregations attempting to make changes on the downside of the life cycle will find it increasingly difficult the further into decline they are.

The case of one congregation on the brink of serious decline demonstrates how a congregation can reset the course of its life cycle. This congregation began by addressing its conflict over a decline in membership and giving and who was at fault in creating that situation. Once the conflict was resolved and members had learned healthy ways of communicating and working together, ideas about what the next phase of their life together might be began to flow. Their first project—to refurbish the youth room—was a test case to see how well they had weathered the conflict and learned new ways of interacting. This involved raising funds, working with the youth and youth minister, hiring contractors, and celebrating the new space when the project was done. The project was a great success. Relationships were rebuilt, and dreams were born out of those relationships. That success led to a willingness to take on bigger challenges. Members had a strong sense that God's Spirit was moving among them, and when the new pastor arrived, they were eager to move forward.

> In transition and change, it is important for leaders to affirm and be pastorally supportive to those who are feeling the loss of what had been.

Since that time, the church has launched several major initiatives, such as making their entire building a green space and going off the electrical grid. As leaders have seen each dream come to fruition, they have already been working on the next dream and planting seeds for it. Their plan is to let the congregation rest and rejuvenate for only a few months between major projects. Leaders worked on new projects as one project ended but didn't launch the next project until the congregation was done celebrating the last one and ready to move into something new. This pattern has allowed people to engage and stay engaged. It has attracted new people to the church, because they see and hear of the great things the church is doing—that the church is addressing real needs of people in the community from a faith-based perspective. People report feeling like they are growing spiritually and making a difference in the world and in the lives of their children. This approach requires a lot of work on the part of leaders, but the longer leaders work at the process, the more second nature it is. The cycle of engagement and rest has affected a complete cultural shift within the congregation.

Such a shift was not without conflict. Some people wanted to go back to the old ways of doing things. Others grieved the loss of a smaller congregation that felt more like a family. In such transition and change, it is important for leaders to affirm and be pastorally supportive to those who are feeling the loss of what had been. The congregation's skills in healthy communication and new ways of working together helped them to hear the concerns but not be paralyzed by them. On the whole, the energy and excitement from the vast majority of members outweighed the naysaying of the few. The obvious growth in members, the congregation's presence in the wider community, and widespread excitement about the vision and ministries of the congregation all provided evidence of a congregation that had come back from the brink of decline and had creatively and imaginatively reinvented itself. God's call was still strong, and listening to that call created a vital, healthy, and thriving congregation that is making a difference in the lives of people inside and outside the congregation.

Recapturing Imagination and Creativity

How does a congregation learn to recapture its imagination and creativity? How do we learn to dream again? The answer partly depends on where the congregation is in its life cycle, what changes are needed, and the conflict that surrounds those changes. However, for most congregations there are a number of basic places to begin.

Learn (or Relearn) to Play

First, the congregation's members need to learn to play together. Many congregations are deadly serious about meetings, projects, and managing the church. We are terrified that the church will collapse if committees and working groups don't meet regularly. We have forgotten how to play and have fun together. We just work and worry, and the working and the worrying seem to beget more worrying. It becomes a vicious cycle and a self-fulfilling prophecy marching toward decline.

Leaders have a role in congregations losing the capacity to play. In the early stages of a congregation's life, leaders are focused on dreaming, building relationships, transforming people's lives, and creating their congregation. They are flexible and playful; that is part of the creating process. The congregation has a strong emphasis on social activities at this stage. People want to be at church because they like each other and want to be together.

As the congregation grows and matures, more structure is needed to carry on the mission of the church. Management is required, and people with skills in organizational development are recruited for this responsibility. As leaders, these people are both visionary and able to create and manage systems to allow the congregation to maximize its mission. Under their care, the congregation is often at its strongest.

As a congregation shifts into its third stage of life, visionary leaders disappear and the managerial leaders become increasingly prominent. Sometimes the visionaries leave the church as it becomes more organized, and sometimes they are simply ready to pass the baton on to a new generation. Once enough managerial leaders are at the forefront, however, the congregation becomes more focused on the systems than on ministry or people, and imagination, creativity, and playfulness recede. The congregation begins to lose flexibility. The congregation becomes less able to tolerate new ideas. If a member has an idea, it has to be vetted by a board or committee and then voted on by a council. By the time an idea is approved

What Does It Mean to Play Together as a Congregation?

Play can happen in a variety of ways. Potluck suppers with a twist like a competition over the best salad or pie or hot dish (I do live in Minnesota!). Themed parties such as a big Mardi Gras festival before Lent. Folk dancing, making art together, sports, picnics—all are ways to play. Even building or fixing up houses or providing supper at a shelter can be ways for the congregation to play and feel like they are giving back, if those activities are done in a spirit of playfulness and community building. There are many ways to play, and the point of it is to build relationships and to enjoy each other.

(or not), the person who proposed it has become frustrated, lost interest, or left to attend another church.

A congregation I worked with hired a young, vibrant pastor, telling him, "We want to grow." But their systems and congregational leaders' control over every decision stymied any efforts at creative thinking. The pastor slowly became frustrated and disillusioned and, not surprisingly, began to look for a new call where his skills and passions would be allowed to flourish and where he could truly grow a congregation. The congregation he left was equally frustrated because they thought it was the pastor's job to grow the church and to do so in a way that didn't require them to do anything. The departed pastor had not been able to help them to realize their role in growth. The congregation wanted to change but were so frightened by the decline around them that they were paralyzed. They would dance toward a new idea and then only half implement it. They restructured the congregation but kept everything essentially the same, just smaller. They didn't free people to dream and run with their passions. The ministry of the church was a ministry of committee meetings with a focus on members themselves and the organization, rather than on the mission they were called to by God. They had ideas, but they were frozen by their fear of dying—and that was quickly becoming a self-fulfilling prophecy.

Learning to play, to let loose of some of the structure and worry, is essential for a congregation to recapture imagination. I have a photograph in my office of a nun in full habit wearing roller skates with a hula-hoop around her waist. Below the picture is an Oscar Wilde quote: "Life is too important to be taken seriously." Sage advice for many of us in congregations! Learning to laugh and particularly laugh at ourselves is critical. We must remember that we are in a partnership with God and it is not all up to us. We need to let God do God's job, while we do ours. We were created to enjoy life. Why else would God have given us the gifts of imagination and creativity?

Take a Break

Another technique for rebuilding energy for creativity and imagination is to take a break. We know the value in our personal lives of taking a break during our work day for a few minutes to clear our minds, breaking for meals, taking a walk to get some fresh air, stopping for a cup of coffee, and of course taking a vacation, though we may tend to work constantly, rarely actually taking time to relax and just be. In the religious world we often talk about observing the Sabbath, but it is rarely practiced in our culture. We have brought into our congregations the bad habit of working all the time. It is why we have trouble playing. It is why we can't take a break from committee meetings. Obviously we have to make sure worship happens and the bills are paid, but many of our churches need to declare a Sabbath and put all nonessential meetings and business on hold. Give the choir a break and sing more hymns in place of anthems. Let the committee work go fallow for a predetermined time to allow energy to be channeled to new and creative thinking.

A church I was a member of sometime ago declared a Sabbath one winter. It was one of the most positive experiences we ever had. People were tired, and getting out of the routine of meetings allowed us to find time to gather for fun and fellowship. We had game nights, movie nights, potlucks, made pizza together, and found multiple ways to enjoy each other's company. The relationships that we built enabled us to return to the "business" of the church with fresh eyes and more creativity. We were able to work together better because we knew each other more deeply. We had friendships. This all enabled us to move the church into new directions for mission, outreach, and growth.

What Does It Look Like to Take a Break as a Congregation?

- Give the choir a break and sing more hymns in place of anthems.

- Let committee work go fallow for a predetermined time to allow energy to be channeled to new and creative thinking.

- Have game nights, movie nights, and potlucks for a season instead of meetings.

- Change an old pattern of doing something, like Sunday school, and find joy and imagination in doing it a new and different way.

Once people are relaxed and able to think instead of react, and enjoy each other while doing so, the opportunity can arise, through a number of methods, to gather those sparks of creativity and imagination. Leaders, of course, will be working throughout the process of leading the congregation and will need to attend to their own needs for play and recreation. But in leading people to play and relax, we are able to then find moments to use that recreation not only for building community, but for preparing people to think more creatively about the mission God has called us to do. Hosting group brainstorming sessions around an area of the congregation's life can be both fun and productive. Take Christian education, for example. What about making Christian education—for children, youth, and adults—more vital and attuned to people's needs? Encourage participants to list every crazy or wild idea. Do not evaluate the ideas; simply generate them. See where this takes you. You may be inspired to rethink what you are doing.

In addition to playing together, another way to take a break is to change an old pattern of doing something and find joy and imagination in doing it a new and different way. For some people, creating something new and different is a playful and invigorating exercise. One congregation I know moved away from Sunday school to an intergenerational Wednesday evening for education and fellowship. They start with a potluck dinner every week and then move into education, community building, and activities that benefit all ages. The Wednesday gathering has been a tremendous success and a time for people to connect with church between Sundays. People not only learn, they have fun and get to know each other. Kids benefit from interacting with people of all ages, not just a Sunday school teacher. Parents get a break because everyone is responsible for the children. Elders interact with and receive care from younger generations and feel less alone. This approach to Christian education meets people's needs in today's world and builds the church at the same time. The new programming has been such a success that it has attracted new people to the congregation.

Evaluate the Pros and Cons

Another way to encourage creative thinking is to list the current practices in an area of the church's life and reflect on the pros and cons for each practice. Examine what is working and what isn't. Take worship, for example, starting with simple things like the time of worship. Is the time a good one, or is it just the time people are used to? Would another time be more convenient and attract more people? What is the worship environment like? Is the sanctuary warm and inviting, or is it formal and set up in a way that makes community difficult to create?

A small congregation I know of had a traditional worship space. Worship leaders struggled to set up their space for worship in a way that was more interactive and community oriented. Their usual arrangement included pews in straight rows and all facing the raised chancel, with an aisle down the middle. The choir sat at the back of the chancel space with the pulpit in front. Congregational leaders created a pros-and-cons list for their existing worship space, and after much conversation and brainstorming, they decided to turn the church sideways. The altar and pulpit are now on one of the long side walls of the sanctuary. All of the pews are in a semicircle facing the altar and pulpit, so worshipers can see each other. The musicians lead from the old chancel but can still interact with the congregation, as only a small portion of the congregation have their backs to them. Worship leaders tend to sit on that side and encourage members to fill the other spaces. The congregation worships in the original space, but the sanctuary looks totally different and meets worshipers' current needs well.

> Often we just go along with what we have always known, rather than considering how we can build on tradition and make worship our own today.

A pros-and-cons list for worship should also consider elements of the service itself. Music, prayers, interaction between leaders and congregation, sermon, style, movement, and a host of other elements should be examined. Often we just go along with what we have always known, rather than considering how we can build on tradition and make worship our own today. As a result, worship seems archaic to many unchurched people. The ritual, style, and substance feel like a holdover from another time and place. For example, the language of traditional hymns doesn't always make sense. I love the hymn "Come, Thou Fount of Every Blessing," but does anyone know what "Here I raise my Ebenezer" means for our lives today?

Another small congregation I worked with wanted to expand the choices of hymns and other worship materials beyond the hymnals in the pews. Leaders were also concerned about the vast amount of paper used every Sunday to create a bulletin, as well as the staff time required to produce the bulletin, especially since the congregation had a small staff with limited hours each week. Their solution after evaluating the pros and cons of their current worship practices and brainstorming ideas was to install two flat-screen monitors in the front of the sanctuary and begin to project the order of worship using the monitors. This allowed worship planners to add hymns, prayers, and litanies that were not in their hymnals. They obtained licenses from various music publishers to legally reproduce the lyrics to the hymns. The monitors also allowed them to use video and other multimedia. They ceased to produce a paper bulletin but did publish a simple one-page announcement sheet for people to take home each week to remind them of activities at the church. This announcement sheet was supplemented by an e-newsletter, a website, and a Facebook page for the congregation. The money saved on paper and time, and because the congregation did not need to purchase additional hymnals or songbooks, more than offset the initial cost of the equipment and the licenses. And the members felt they had made a substantial environmental contribution.

> Use positive techniques that aim to build on what is working rather than focusing on what's broken.

Use Facilitated Brainstorming Techniques

Asset mapping, force-field analysis, and mind mapping are facilitated brainstorming techniques your congregation can use to identify its assets as well as tap into the leaders' and members' creative energy. These three techniques focus on the positive and aim to build on what is working rather than focusing on what's broken.

Asset-based community development grew out of the work of John P. Kretzmann and John L. McKnight at Northwestern University. They founded the Asset-Based Community Development Institute to help communities find ways to grow and thrive. Luther K. Snow, a faith-based trainer and community organizer for the Evangelical Lutheran Church in

America and now a private consultant, built on the technique to create asset mapping.[2] He honed his technique working in rural communities with small congregations, helping them rethink who they are and what God is calling them to do using the assets they already possess. This is key because so many congregations believe they have no gifts and no assets.

My maxim is that God has given each congregation what it needs to fulfill our calling at this time. I learned this from one of my mentors, Patrick Keifert, and it has proven true time and again. So the central question for congregations is, What is God calling your congregation to do and be right now? If you can discern that, then you will also discover you have the gifts and assets you need to get you going. Asset mapping is an excellent tool for doing just that. The congregation described earlier that created a multifamily housing complex used asset mapping to determine that the single-family dwelling they had used for refugee resettlement sat on a piece of property that could accommodate a larger housing complex and serve many more families, including refugees and working homeless people. They had the asset. They just needed a vision.

> What is God calling your congregation to do and be right now? If you can discern that, then you will also discover you have the gifts and assets you need to get you going.

Asset mapping. Asset mapping is a fairly simple process. According to Snow, you begin with everyone writing down any assets the congregation has.[3] These assets can be physical, individual, or economic. The assets can also be things like associations with other individuals or groups or institutions. Each person writes down assets—one asset per piece of paper—and these are shared in small groups and then posted on the wall. The next step is to begin to cluster assets that form action ideas, not similar or alike assets. The clusters must be action-oriented and in line with what the group believes God is calling the congregation to do. Finally, the group prioritizes the actions by physically standing next to the cluster that they want to get involved with. The task is very clearly about getting involved. The outcome should be a list of two or three actions based on the assets of the congregation to send people out in mission.

Force-field analysis. Force-field analysis is a tried and true technique that is not often used anymore but should be. Developed by social psychologist Kurt Lewin, the technique uncovers those forces that maintain the status quo and keep congregations from realizing our dreams or ideas. It is similar to a pros-and-cons list, but the lists are constructed by matching the pros and cons to show how specific cons are keeping the pros from moving the congregation forward.

The force-field analysis is set up with three columns on a flipchart pad or a whiteboard. The middle column represents the idea or project you want to enact. The first column represents those positive forces that would enable you to succeed with the project. The third column is opposing or

Action-Oriented Asset Clusters

Once you have a collection of assets, create clusters that form action ideas that are in line with what the group believes God is calling the congregation to do. Here is an example of an asset cluster from the church that created the housing project:

- Asset: Large piece of property at the north end of the parking lot

- Asset: Montessori school as one of the church's ministries that could accommodate more children

- Asset: Church members with knowledge of building and managing rental properties

- Asset: Good working relationship with interfaith housing agency

- Asset: Several members with solid political connections to city and state elected officials

Putting all those together, it was easy to connect the dots into the action of creating a multifamily housing complex to serve families that are working but cannot afford traditional rent or mortgages.

negative forces to each positive force. These are the forces that maintain the status quo, hindering forward movement or change. The goal is to build up the positive forces and weaken the negative forces to the point that the positives overwhelm the negatives and move an idea or project to success. It is a visual way to think through a problem and how to move beyond the negatives to a positive outcome.

We saw an example of such a shift in the story about the congregation that made major changes in the way they handled weddings and the signing of marriage licenses and weathered a small group of naysayers who tried to disrupt the forward movement. The small group could have disrupted the old system and made it stall, at a minimum, or sent it into a tailspin, at a maximum. But the changes the congregation put into place, the communication guidelines that were functioning, and the new learned behaviors on how to be community together allowed this congregation to hear and see the tactics of the naysayers, minimizing their negative impact and keeping the congregation moving forward on its new course.

Mind mapping. A final technique—mind mapping—is a creative, fun, and organized way to use free association to visually capture a group's thinking. Rooted in ancient philosophy, the technique has become quite elaborate over time. However, you can begin simply. The method requires a large piece of paper or a white- or blackboard. In the center of the space, draw a circle or square and write the primary idea you are going to mind map in that circle or square. Let's take outreach as a topic. The next step is to begin drawing branches off the center, each representing a primary idea in the category of outreach. These might be possibilities like advocacy, direct service, and fundraising, or they might include areas for engagement like homelessness, literacy, and public policy. You continue to draw more branches off each of the primary branches as a way to identify ideas to explore. When the mind map is finished, it looks similar to a spider, with the central idea as the body and all the subsequent possible avenues for enacting the main idea shooting off the center like legs of the spider.

A mind map is a visual way to brainstorm. The technique is to keep drawing more branches, without stopping to evaluate them, until the ideas are exhausted. Then you can go back and begin to explore and evaluate.

The value of the mind map is that it creates a visual beyond a list and it connects the various ideas in pathways. Lists do not enable us to readily make these sorts of connections. In my experience, most groups that experiment with mind mapping are shocked at the wealth of ideas they possess and the new avenues they identify for exploration.

We were created to imagine, dream, and create. Using those gifts is critical to solving the either/or dilemma that keeps us living in the extremes. These gifts give us options and choices from which to discern God's call.

If your congregation needs a consultant to teach any of these techniques, your denominational leaders, a nearby seminary, or a ministry development center might be good sources for facilitators or be able to refer you to facilitators. Other resources include ecumenical church support organizations such as the Center for Progressive Renewal or Congregational Consulting, which is composed of consultants from the former Alban Institute. You may also contact me about consulting possibilities.

Managing Polarities

Some situations, however, are not a matter of just creating new options or choices. Some situations demand we learn to recognize and negotiate between the extremes if we are to thrive as a congregation. Both poles of a polarity are true and, to an extent, desirable responses to the same question. They seem to be opposites, potentially excluding the other, but they are both in fact necessary to provide the balance and direction a congregation needs.

> We were created to imagine, dream, and create. Using those gifts is critical to solving the either/or dilemma that keeps us living in the extremes.

A simple example is the polarity of innovation versus tradition in worship. Many congregations do not want to lose touch with our traditions and at the same time know we must innovate and offer worship that touches people today. If a congregation completely abandons tradition in worship, we lose both our mooring and often our older members. This happened in my parents' church, where the worship planners abandoned traditional hymnody for contemporary pop-style music. The younger generations may have liked the new style of music, but they were missing a significant part of the history of the church in not learning and appreciating older hymns. And the older members felt it a slap in the face to all their years of worshipping to lose this important dimension. Another example is churches in the 1960s and '70s that substituted donuts and coffee for bread and wine at communion. This may have been more emblematic of the times, but it quickly faded as a fad that wasn't faithful to the tradition's understanding of what Jesus did at the Last Supper. Managing the polarities in cases like these requires learning to incorporate the best of the old with the best of the new, creating worship that speaks across generations and preserves both tradition and innovation.

Barry Johnson, who developed polarity management in 1975 and founded Polarity Partnerships, translates the either/or dilemma from "I'm right and you are wrong!" versus "No, I'm right and you are wrong!" to "We are both right given certain circumstances and both wrong in other circumstances."

When faced with polarities, both parties are both right and wrong—right in that both have identified a truth that, if it triumphs over the other and is adopted as the sole solution, will be wrong. Polarities require both/and thinking, rather than a more easily defined dichotomy of either/or.

> Navigating back and forth between the poles of tradition and innovation, managing and leading, caring for members and reaching out to the world around us are all aspects of a strong and vital congregation.

In an either/or situation, one end may or may not be true. When a congregation says, "We must do this or we will die" or "If we change, we will be untrue to who we are," these statements are not necessarily true. However, there comes a point in a congregation's life cycle when it requires the flexibility and looseness of creativity *and* the structure that comes with managerial expertise. Flexible creativity and structured management seem like opposites, but without both ends of the spectrum, a congregation will lack balance and become unsustainable.

Roy M. Oswald of the former Alban Institute teamed up with Johnson to produce *Managing Polarities in Congregations: Eight Keys for Thriving Faith Communities*. In it they detail eight key polarities that must be managed for congregations to thrive. These are as follows:

1. Tradition *and* Innovation
2. Spiritual Health *and* Institutional Health
3. Management *and* Leadership
4. Strong Clergy Leadership *and* Strong Lay Leadership
5. Inreach *and* Outreach
6. Nurture *and* Transformation
7. Making Disciples: Easy Process *and* Challenging Process
8. Call *and* Duty [4]

Johnson explains that the polarity management process is like breathing. We must both inhale and exhale or we cannot breathe. Without exhaling, inhaling will eventually hurt us. Likewise, exhaling is no good without inhaling. Managing a polarity works the same way. Each pole contributes to a situation, and each has negative aspects. We loop back and forth between the poles to take advantage of the positive aspects of both poles and minimize the negative.

Johnson describes this motion as an infinity loop. He illustrates the motion on a four-quadrant map with each pole of the polarity at one end of a horizontal axis. At each pole, the positive aspects of that pole are listed above the horizontal axis, and the negative aspects are listed below, forming a quadrant. When people identify a problem with one pole, the solution is to move to the positive aspect of the opposite pole.

The key is to learn to manage adeptly on the positive sides of both poles, minimizing the downsides, and not careening back and forth. In fact, Johnson says, "In a well-managed polarity most time is spent experiencing the positive aspects of one pole or the other. When the downside of a pole is experienced, it is used as a signal to move to the positive of the other pole."[5]

Congregations need to develop a healthy notion of risk taking and also manage the emotions present in the system. This is where a calm, nonanxious presence is absolutely necessary. Leaders are always navigating back and forth between the poles of the polarity. They are mindful of the value of both tradition and innovation, being both a manager and a leader, having both strong clergy and strong lay leadership, both caring for the congregation and reaching out to the world around it. These are all aspects of a strong and vital congregation. The key is not one or the other. It is both/and.

One congregation I worked with intensely had reached a point in its life where members were exploding with innovative ideas, and the church's programming and outreach were growing by leaps and bounds, but they were tied to a fairly traditional organizational and governance structure that no longer served them.

Opportunities for children, youth, and adults in spiritual formation were strong. Social activities within the congregation for building community were well attended. People were engaged in direct service and advocacy projects that addressed homelessness, health care, and education. Members felt renewed energy for upgrading a more traditional nursery school program into a full-fledged early childhood education center. The congregation was attracting a significant number of new members. And new ideas kept coming as people enjoyed the thriving congregation.

But the structure of the congregation no longer served this thriving situation. It inhibited people from getting involved. People had to go through multiple layers of approval if they wanted to implement an idea. Rather than get bogged down in bureaucracy, people began to circumvent the governance structure and just enacted their plans or took their suggestions directly to the whole congregation. The system became more nonfunctional because the most exciting projects in the congregation were happening outside of the governance structure. The nominating committee was unable to fill positions on all the committees and boards, because people wanted to get involved in the ministry of the congregation rather than attend meetings and serve on committees. Once this situation was noticed, leaders revealed that the nominating committee hadn't been able to present a full slate of candidates for ten years. They also documented that a significant number of people who said yes to being

> People want to get involved in the ministry of the congregation rather than attend meetings and serve on committees.

nominated never finished their terms of office. They were still in the congregation and still active but didn't want to serve in management.

One constitutionally created board voted itself out of existence, even though they didn't have the authority to take that action. Its members were tired of meeting each month and losing time away from the exciting ministries they were supposed to be overseeing. People wondered aloud if it wasn't time to allow the staff to do more of the day-to-day management of the congregation and let the members engage more in ministry.

After a long period of growing frustration and frequent conversation, the congregation voted to radically alter its governance structure. Members kept the council—three new members each year for three-year terms—and the nominating committee. All other committees and boards became ad hoc. Many committees, such as Christian education and stewardship, continued to exist, but members no longer had to be nominated to be part of the committee or hold an office. The council was substantially reduced in size, to nine members from around twenty, to make it more nimble and flexible. The council no longer needed to include representatives from committees or boards. The members of the council were charged with visioning for the church, setting policy and procedure, and setting the course for the staff and the congregation based on the mission and vision statements along with the priorities adopted by the congregation at the annual meeting each year. These priorities addressed one goal for church organizational life, one goal for church spiritual life, and one goal for the church's engagement in the life of the community.

While the new structure was hard for some of the longtime members of the congregation to adjust to, it was generally well received as people began to focus more on the ministries of the church and less and less on meetings. People began to enjoy the freedom to develop projects and ministries around ideas they felt led to propose. Staff members were happier, because they got to use their gifts more in the new system. They spent less time trying to motivate committees and more time in ministry. There were bugs to work out in the new system along the way, but overall it gave the congregation a radically different governance and organizational structure that served the growing ministries of the congregation. It balanced and managed a critical polarity, the need for both thriving and creative leadership *and* structure and management for the programs created.

The Polarity of Church and Culture

Congregations face other polarities in addition to those on Oswald's list. A primary one is learning to manage the reality of the culture as unchurched and the reality of the church needing and wanting to exist and thrive in an unwelcoming culture. While this polarity may push the bounds of the polarity definition a bit—the culture is not an internal entity over which the church has any control—it is nevertheless a reality. While the church throughout history has always had to manage between the culture and the church, the balance tipped in 312. Constantine converted to Christianity and it became culturally and legally the official religion of the Holy Roman Empire. Until recently the church has been dominant in Western culture and negotiated with that culture from a position of dominance. We now manage from a nondominant position and must determine how to thrive when we are unable to control or even significantly influence the culture.

If congregational leaders are willing to be thoughtful and reconsider the current situation, it can become a great opportunity. This is a place for our creativity and imagination to flourish, if we are willing to take a deep breath, have courage, and move forward. It is exactly in this space, which can seem hopeless, that the church can most easily sense the movement of God. We can capture a new vision of doing things, a new way that God is calling us into for this time and this place.

An excellent example of reconsidering what appears to be a negative situation and imaginatively creating an opportunity is a congregation that had once been thriving in its small town. As time went by, the town, and with it the congregation, began to shrink. The church—I'll call it "Community Church"—went from being a fairly large and bustling place to a small and struggling gathering. The town's change in demographics and size, coupled with the changing attitude of the culture that de-emphasized church and allowed for greater competition with church left Community Church wondering if it would even survive.

Community Church began a visioning process to reinvent itself, as members decided the only way the congregation could survive would be to come to terms with their current reality, accepting that the community had changed and wasn't going back to the way it used to be. They accepted they would be smaller, given the circumstances of their town. They chose to share a pastor with a church in a nearby town to keep their costs in line with their budget. They decided to focus on their current strengths—in their case, music—rather than trying to do everything they had traditionally done.

They focused on the musical dimensions of worship and also began to offer community concerts featuring other musicians from the area. This approach began to draw people who had never considered going to Community Church. The offering collections at the concerts began to significantly supplement their budget.

> If congregational leaders are willing to be thoughtful and reconsider the current situation, it can become a great opportunity. It is exactly in this space, which can seem hopeless, that the church can most easily sense the movement of God.

In order to manage between a changing culture and the survival and hopeful thriving of the congregation, Community Church had to completely rethink who it was and accept what would never be again. Working through that process and continuing to think in new and different ways was essential to its successful navigation of the polarity they were trapped in. The congregation is now considering hiring a youth minister who is bilingual in Spanish, given that their community has a growing Latino population. Considering a bilingual ministry is markedly different from how they had understood themselves, but leaders recognize an exciting new opportunity to serve in their community. Community Church will probably never be a booming congregation again, but it is a vital one that serves its community well and responds to the mission and call of God. As leaders continue to manage the loop between congregation and culture, they are discovering an exciting journey.

Key for any congregation that is seeking to manage polarities, address conflict, and thrive in change is to examine the stories we tell about ourselves. These narratives are critical to successfully navigating the realities of congregational life. Stories enable us to envision who we are and reframe issues that might prevent us from dealing with the constant change we face. The stories also help us understand God's interaction with us and with people of faith since the beginning of human history. We turn now to story and the role of narrative in congregations.

Reflecting on Your Congregation . . .

1. Make a list: If I allowed myself to let go of things (programs, policies, structures) in my congregation, I would . . .

2. About what topics do you say, "If we only had or did this" or "I dream about us doing or having that"?

3. Whether you are a pastor or a lay leader, start a list of dreams for your congregation. What are some strategies you could use to make some of those dreams come true?

4. Where is your congregation in its life cycle?

    What does this mean for your congregation?

    How would your congregation need to change to move from quadrant 3 or 4 and begin a new life cycle?

5. How does your congregation play and how often?

    Compare the number of hours in meetings with those you spend playing and those in worship. Is the balance what you need or want?

6. Think of a current problem or conflict. Are people talking in either/or categories?

    If so, how might you help them break out of that thinking and be more imaginative about solutions?

7. What is one strategy you'd like to try from this chapter?

    Regarding what situation?

    Carefully consider in what setting this might be fruitful to experiment with.

What Is Our Story?

Discovering and Changing the Way We See Ourselves

The more I listened, the more I understood the unfolding story of the congregation. It was a small, struggling inner-city congregation whose longtime members, upper-middle-class professionals, were becoming retirees with less disposable income. The new members were primarily young families who had not yet reached their full earning potential. The funds bequeathed to the congregation by deceased members had not always been handled with an eye to the future. Leaders had used some of the money as it came in, and the congregation was now facing a looming financial crisis. On top of the financial challenges, the church had limited parking, which served as a major impediment to growth.

The biggest issue facing this congregation, however, was an identity crisis: members didn't know what their mission was and what they wanted to do. They did what "churches" do, and they did it as a family. But just like many families, they had their dysfunctions. They were not open to new folks, and they had no idea how to work together, to find a balance among the roles of the pastor, lay leaders, and members.

Their long-term pastor had overfunctioned, doing nearly everything for the congregation, from making sure the boiler worked to preaching to organizing events and activities to pastoral care work and visitation to community outreach. The less the congregation's members did for themselves, the more the pastor picked up and filled the vacuum. This arrangement would probably have continued except for a devastating depression and nervous breakdown that forced the pastor to retire. This abrupt change was difficult for the pastor and his family, and the congregation took his illness hard and was lost in a sea of guilt, shame, anger, and grief.

In the interim period before calling a new pastor, the congregation worked to understand how it had contributed to this tragic situation, and the pendulum swung the other way. When the next pastor was called, he significantly underfunctioned, and the congregation picked up the slack. The pastor preached and led worship but did virtually no pastoral care and provided little leadership to the congregation or the staff. Congregational leaders struggled with when and how to tell him it was time he moved on. He saved them the trouble and accepted a call from another congregation. People were happy for him and relieved that they could now move into another phase of the congregation's life. They just didn't know what that was or how to go about it.

> To understand a congregation, leaders need to know how to look for clues that unveil the systems and metaphors that drive its story.

This congregation's internal problems were systemic. The system had allowed for extreme overfunctioning in one long-term pastorate and significant underfunctioning in another, shorter pastorate. The congregation had responded accordingly, moving from extreme underfunctioning to significant overfunctioning. Members admitted they weren't sure what normal functioning was. They knew they were tired. They knew they needed leadership, but they were having trouble letting go.

Three major forces were at work in this congregation and appear in many others like it. First, the system was out of balance, and leaders did not understand how systems work. Second, the metaphors of the congregation as family and church as home pointed to not only a closed system, but also a potentially damaging way of understanding themselves and their potential for attracting new members. And finally, their shortcomings had found their way into the story they kept telling themselves about who they were. This narrative of the broken, declining church that had nearly killed a pastor haunted them and their perception of themselves. As one person said to me, "It is past time for us to let go of that story and stop carrying it around."

Every congregation has a system that dictates how it functions (or doesn't function!) in times of change and conflict. And every congregation has metaphors it uses to describe its life together. And finally, every congregation has a story or stories that members tell themselves and others. These three elements are vital to understand if we are to manage the journey of a congregation through the ups and downs of change and conflict. In many ways the story most clearly conveys what is going on. To understand a congregation, leaders need to know how to look for clues that unveil the systems and metaphors that drive its story.

Systems in Congregations

There was a day and age when management and leadership theory presented organizations as machines. A legacy of the Industrial Age, this viewpoint influenced the church leadership and management literature as well. Organizations' goal was to function like a well-oiled, smoothly running piece of equipment. The strategy was to keep the discrete parts of the congregation functioning well, because the congregational "machine" would cease to function if one part was broken. This mechanistic view led leaders and managers to focus on each part of the organization and to examine the connections between the parts in their individual functions. There was no thought given to the whole mechanism or the effect of the individual parts on the whole machine. The parts were much more important than the whole.

Yet congregations, like other organizations, are human driven and a great deal more complex than even the most sophisticated machine. Congregations operate as a whole system, but they are not neat and orderly. Within the main system a complex web of subsystems may or may not share the same goals. The way these subsystems work together helps to determine the difference between a healthy and thriving congregation and an unhealthy and dysfunctional congregation.

Healthy and thriving congregations that weather conflict and change well are able to find a balance between internal needs and outward mission. They do not overemphasize one or the other. They create a strong education program for children, youth, and adults, as well as outreach in various mission opportunities. They have an effective governance system and dream and discern the next task God is calling the congregation to do. They offer opportunities for community building through fun activities and for service together. And of course, they gather for engaging and meaningful worship that speaks to the lives of people today. No congregation perfectly manages all of this 100 percent of the time, but thriving congregations get there most of the time. A healthy system allows them to do so.

Closed Systems versus Open Systems

To identify the source of a congregation's weaknesses, observers need to determine if the congregation is operating as a closed system or an open system. Closed systems have clear boundaries marking what belongs to the system and what is outside the system. There is little interaction between the system and the surrounding environment. The goals of a closed system are to take only what is needed for survival from the environment and to protect the system from harmful elements in that environment. Machines are generally closed systems. They are self-contained and do not interact with or take information or anything else from the environment around them. Human organizations such as bureaucracies tend to be closed systems, refusing to be influenced by, gain information from, or interact with other organizations outside of themselves.

The family is often seen as a closed system. To be part of a family system, one must be born, adopted, or married into a family. The system draws boundaries around who is formally in the family. Many factors influence whether a family system is functional or dysfunctional. Addiction and mental illness can disrupt a family system. So can abuse. And often, due to the closed nature of the family system, the very elements that turn a family into a dysfunctional system are kept as secrets within the system. Further, members of the system are unwilling to allow outside intervention to help get the family back on track. The warped understanding of family that develops accompanies members of the family into the world around them and affects all the relationships of which they are a part, including the church.

Open systems, by contrast, have permeable boundaries. Open systems interact with their environments both as a matter of survival and to ensure they can become vital and thriving. For instance, our bodies are open systems. Yes, they appear to be closed. We can clearly say what belongs to our bodies and what the boundaries of our bodies are. But our boundaries, physically and psychically, are porous. A healthy immune system seeks to eliminate harmful elements from our bodies in order to prevent disease, but admits elements that are helpful to us. We interact with the environment to get nutrients we need for survival—consider the vitamin D we glean from sunshine. Sometimes we interact with the environment to our detriment—think recreational drug use.

Congregations can choose to be open or closed systems. The church has its greatest potential when it functions as an open system, but we often operate as if it were a closed system. We fail to look at ourselves in a holistic manner. We do not see that if the ushers fail to greet visitors warmly on Sunday morning, that affects how newcomers perceive our hospitality and may discourage them from joining, thus leading to continued decline from lack of new members. This is but one example of how a seemingly small part of the system impacts the larger system and defeats our goals. We often do not perceive our self-defeating behaviors that either drive people away or discourage them from joining us in the first place. We turn inward, seeing ourselves as complete and not needing to be open to what is happening in the outside world.

> Congregations can choose to be open or closed systems. The church has its greatest potential when we function as an open system, but we often operate as if we were closed.

A clear example of the effect one area of a church's life can have on another is the congregation where I was ordained (discussed in chapter 2). It was a small congregation with a substantial endowment that allowed it to keep going despite fairly empty pews on Sundays. When the church finally attracted a couple of talented and energetic pastors, they began to attract new people who were different from most of the longtime members. A real us-versus-them mentality began to develop.

As mentioned earlier, the new members began to work for changes that opened the congregation up to the needs of people around the city where the church was located. Ideas abounded and a portion of the congregation became more excited about the possibilities. But the old guard positioned itself on the board, which controlled the money, and effectively shut down all new ideas. The excitement was squelched by frustration, and conflict began to arise.

In addition to learning the history of the church and being bolstered by the congregation's own history, the newcomers along with the pastors began to organize. They began to ensure new members and sympathetic longtime members filled seats on key committees and boards. They strategized about congregational meetings and took control of the agenda. They called people, encouraged them to attend important meetings, and prepared them to really engage with the ideas and possibilities of the church. Finally, they began to work on breaking up the small group of approximately five to seven longtime members who were preventing the congregation from moving forward. They eventually asked the leader of the old guard to leave because of his behavior, which included physically intimidating one of the pastors. This finally freed the congregation for the possibility of a new future, even though that effort to reclaim control of the congregation took a heavy toll on the members and the pastors. No one had any energy left to begin a vision for something new. It took a while to rebuild the congregation, but it is now moving in different and good directions.

Because the various parts were unable to work together as a whole, this congregation had to act much like an immune system in the body and drive out harmful elements. The question that must be addressed in a conflict such as this is, What is best for the congregation as a whole? This is systems thinking. If a person is acting out, as in the earlier examples, the needs of the one are not more important than those of the whole. We may respond pastorally to someone acting out, but the needs of the whole congregation or committee are often more important than one individual's. Sometimes the situation can be contained and the individual worked with to bring the person around for the good of the whole. Other times the individual must be removed from the committee, group, or even the congregation to protect the needs of the whole. Removing a member or leader is particularly difficult for many pastors and lay leaders. We are all too often willing to let the needs of one person or a small group of people dictate the course of the whole. This does not serve anyone well, nor is it faithful leadership.

Metaphors as Keys to Understanding

Metaphors are exceedingly helpful clues to what is going on in a congregation, because they shape the story the congregation is telling about ourselves, and the story becomes our reality. As we know, the language of theology is a language of metaphors: God is Father, Peter was a rock, and God's people are sheep. None of these is literally true, but as metaphors, they express ideas that are hard to explain or that we want to more deeply understand.

Metaphors in the life of a congregation are often biblical in nature. The church is the body of Christ. The church is the bride of Christ. The church is polis (from our earlier exploration of Philippians). The church is a family. The church is the army of God. The church is a royal priesthood. The church is a sanctuary. The church is the hands and feet of God in the world.

All of these, plus others, have been used at various times and places to describe the church, and some have fallen out of fashion. In a contemporary world, we do not use the image of the bride of Christ often. The implications of the metaphor do not make sense given the understandings of marriage, gender roles, and various Christologies operating in churches. It feels awkward and antiquated in today's world and church. Likewise, the church as the army of God is uncomfortable for churches that seek to offer a message of peace to the world. Being seen or seeing themselves as God's soldiers contradicts the message they wish to communicate.

> If people come from a family that is unhealthy and we tell them they are part of a family at church, they will act in the only way they know how to act in a family.

The church as family is a popular metaphor for many different traditions. Yet as the discussion of closed systems indicates, this metaphor can create difficulties for congregations. It tends to indicate the congregation has an internal focus and often lacks a sense of call in mission. The church as family can feel to newcomers like a clique or a collection of cliques. The newcomers are outside the system, not part of the immediate family. The family members, more interested in each other, are polite to newcomers but essentially ignore them. And sometimes newcomers are treated with disdain. A "Who are you?" attitude can prevail that makes visitors think twice about returning.

Finding a new church to join when my spouse and I moved to a new city proved daunting to me. It became very clear that we were outsiders and not part of the family of the congregations we visited. We visited a dozen or so churches, and in all but two we were completely ignored. People in one were friendly, and we ended up joining that congregation. In the other, the pastor was welcoming and introduced us to some folks at coffee hour. They talked to us long enough to be polite, but soon we were left standing alone, yet again. We received a stark lesson in the closed systems of multiple congregations. These were not families that welcomed in strangers and newcomers.

Using family as a metaphor for church often transfers a level of dysfunction from home to church. If people come from a family that is unhealthy and we tell them they are part of a family at church, they will act in the only way they know how to act in a family.

With the metaphors and systems understood, we can now begin to look to stories congregations tell ourselves. The stories are shaped by the system and the metaphors and tell us the mission, vision, and possibilities for a congregation. These are the elements that help a congregation weather conflict and change because the congregation is following the call of God as we seek to be salt, light (see, we can't get away from metaphors!), and hope to a world in need of God's love, peace, justice, and joy.

The Importance of Story

Congregations create stories to explain who and what we are. These stories often have some dimension of truth, but ultimately they are interpretations of truth. As a congregation tries to move forward into the future, those interpretations will affect our success for good or ill.

The growing understanding of the importance of narrative in healing from the past and building toward a new imagined future—a preferred future with a vision of God's desire for us—provides an important tool and strategy for congregations emerging from conflict. Telling our story allows us to become stronger and clearer about who we are and what God is calling us to do.

Having worked a great deal with small congregations—rural, suburban, and urban—I have heard a lot of statements such as "We are losers," "We can't get a 'real' pastor [meaning a man with wife and children in tow] because we are so small," "We used to be great, but now we can barely keep the lights on. It is depressing." It saddens me to hear these stories.

One congregation stands out in my experiences as a consultant. "St. Luke's" was founded in a strong farming community at a time when family farms and related industries were booming. Slowly this way of life had changed as family farm after family farm was sold to conglomerates, and the community had shifted. Further, many farming communities had lost many of their young people after they finished college. There were no jobs to return to, so slowly the community dwindled. St. Luke's sat on the cusp, however, of a new phenomenon. The nearby city, which used to seem far away, had slowly been growing toward them. Some of the old farms were being transformed by developers into suburban neighborhoods and were attracting young families who commuted into the city for work. This was not a reality St. Luke's was prepared to address.

> Telling our story allows us to become stronger and clearer about who we are and what God is calling us to do.

One of the times I was with them, one of the older members proudly showed me their beautiful building. They had kept the building up, and it was pristine. After our consulting sessions were completed, this same member came up and asked me what I thought of the church. I thought she was still referring to the building and replied that it was a beautiful church. "No," she said. "I didn't mean the building. I meant us. Are we okay?" She was sad in responding to my misunderstanding. I began to realize what low self-esteem this congregation was experiencing.

As I travelled home, I thought back through all the various conversations we had had together over the course of the consultation as the congregation's story had slowly emerged. These were proud people who had worked hard all their lives. They had memories of a beautiful church in the middle of their farms that was packed every Sunday. Their world and their church had changed, but the story now was one of loss and a deep fear that somehow they had done something wrong and were being punished as they watched their church slowly dwindle and die.

The story they wanted to believe was that they were still that big, beautiful country church that reflected their heritage as immigrant farmers. The reality was that they weren't that church anymore. And the current story of the church—we are not okay, we are wrong, we are sad, we are dying—continued to get in the way of creating a new story of the church that could be. These narrative refrains deeply affected their ability to let go into a new future and to attract new members into their midst. No one wants to be part of a church that sees itself as a community of losers with low self-esteem. Without a new story, this congregation would make its fears that it was a dying congregation a self-fulfilling prophecy.

The Theology and Therapy of Narrative Thinking

Narrative thinking in congregations is rooted in two disciplines. First, narrative theology traces its history back to the work of H. Richard Niebuhr and the lineage that developed from his work through other diverse theologians. The goal of narrative theology is to look for the theology embedded in the faith journeys of people, as opposed to developing a set of doctrinal principles that are meant to apply to everyone and every circumstance. Of course, the biblical narrative is the foundation and ultimate narrative of God's interaction with humankind. While our own stories don't carry the same weight as biblical narratives, narrative theology affirms that valuable theological insights can be found in the faith journeys of groups of people, such as congregations. In my earlier story of the church whose definition of church was "Happy + Nice," I arrived at a theological conclusion for that congregation based on listening to their stories. In this case, their stories pointed to an inadequate theological principle that was contributing to the dysfunction of their congregation.

> Narrative theology looks for the theology embedded in the faith journeys of people, as opposed to developing a set of doctrinal principles that are meant to apply to everyone and every circumstance.

The second discipline underlying narrative thinking is that of narrative therapy, which traces its roots to the work of Michael White and David Epston in the 1970s and 1980s, and the publication of their book *Narrative Means to Therapeutic Ends* in 1990. Narrative therapy seeks to discover the meaning of people's lives and the solutions to the problems people face through the stories of people's lives. It takes a nonjudgmental and collaborative approach to therapy that separates people from their problems and sees them as the experts on their own lives. It opens the door for the therapist to work closely with the client to uncover the stories and their meanings and thus to aid in clients understanding their lives.

These two disciplines are in conversation with each other largely through the medium of pastoral counseling. They also have implications for leadership, congregational culture, congregational change, and even pastoral formation.

The Power of Story on Perspective

The former Alban Institute and Virginia Theological Seminary, with the support of the Luce Foundation, conducted the Narrative Leadership Project. Building on the narrative movement as it has developed in psychology, education, organizational development, literature, history, biblical studies, and other disciplines, such as Ronald Heifetz's work on adaptive leadership, the project sought to explore "the power of story retrieval, reconstruction, and presentation as a framework for ministry, leadership, and congregational change." The project saw that "the potential of an overarching narrative framework for ministry has yet to be tapped."[1]

The insights of their work affirmed the discoveries I had been making in my work with a variety of congregations as pastor, denominational executive, teacher, and consultant. Story is a powerful tool in both understanding a congregation and making changes in that congregation. It can shape the future of the congregation for ill if we choose not to address the negative themes the narrative reveals. The story can also give clues when discerning the call of God for our new and thriving future. The story can show that God is not done with many congregations that are afraid the future is one of slow decline.

Churches that believe we are "losers" or "cannot get a real pastor" will eventually die if we do not change our story. This requires first recognizing the themes and patterns of the current story. Once that story is recognized, members need to understand the various stories over their lifespan, as well as relate the current story to the biblical narrative and the stories of the congregation over time. Congregations need a sense of where we fit into the larger narrative of the Christian faith and the history of our community. This is not to glorify the past but to locate the church in the scheme of things. The final step for the congregation is to dream and discern a new trajectory in order to create a new story with new metaphors, built on past traditions but not wedded to them in a way that drags us back into the past. This is hard but rewarding work. This is also faithful work. Every congregation must redefine the faith and our mission for the day and age we are in, not the past. We most honor those who came before us when we act as boldly as they did.

Story is a powerful tool in understanding and making changes in a congregation. It shapes our future, gives clues for discerning the call of God, and can show that God is not done with us when we are afraid our future is one of slow decline.

Diana Butler Bass uses a wonderful comparison in her essay "Living the Story." She references the fact that many mainline churches use the metaphor of the Titanic to illustrate their current state of affairs. Often people will say they feel like they are "rearranging the deck chairs on the Titanic" when they are making changes in the church. This metaphor portends the doom and gloom ahead for these churches. They are sinking. They are dying. There is no hope.

Butler Bass proposes congregations instead draw on the metaphor of the Mayflower. The Mayflower was a ship making a journey fraught with difficulties and danger as it carried the Pilgrims across the Atlantic to their home in the New World. But despite the difficulties and dangers, the journey of the Mayflower was one of hope, a call from God to a new place to be church. They eagerly anticipated what was to come, even though no one knew what that would be or what it would look like. They weren't feeling dread and fear that ultimately no matter what they did, the ship was going to sink.[2] To find hope in the midst of uncertainty is the power of the story.

Recognizing Your Story

Discovering your congregation's story is a bit like being a detective. The clues are there; you just have to find them. One of the easiest ways to access clues is to listen to the way people talk about the church. What metaphors do they use? Are they always talking about the past? Do they express dreams and hopes? Fear and apprehension about the future? Do they refer to one moment as special or to a time when they were great? The language we use reveals what we believe about ourselves, and what we believe about ourselves is tied up with our story.

A second way to access the story of a church is to poke around in the closets—the literal closets and the figurative closets—to see what is hiding there. What are the inglorious moments people want to hide? What sorts of stuff has been hidden away, out of sight? I looked in the literal closets of one church to find some interesting sculptures. I suggested that since this congregation loved art, we should display them. Then the stories tumbled out about who had given them and the negative backstory connected with them. They represented a little piece of the troubled past of what was at that time a troubled congregation. Our past is never far behind our present, especially if the past was difficult and not dealt with. For this congregation, once the ghosts of the past had been confronted, the conversation turned from members not wanting to display the sculptures because they brought up bad memories to an aesthetic discussion that was much healthier.

Even more difficult to explore are the figurative closets. These are the places we hide all the stories we don't want to see the light of day—bad things, shameful things, and things that we thought we had long ago banished. The first case of clergy sexual misconduct I dealt with involved an associate pastor arrested for sexual acts with children in the neighborhood surrounding the church. I was part of a team that went into the church in the aftermath to try to help the congregation deal with the news. We went in prepared for conversation about the stories of this minister and their church that were hitting the daily papers. Instead, what we heard about was an incident from about forty years prior when the minister ran off with the organist. The theory about how to deal with such problems at the time that incident happened was "out of sight, out of mind." Members felt a great deal of shame that this had happened in their church, and all the shame and anger burst out of its figurative closet door with the new incident before them. We were not prepared for what we heard, but we dealt with it. I have since had that same experience of a current situation opening the way for all the ghost stories of the past to come out. And until they do, they lie there festering and affecting the current life of the congregation.

A third way to discover clues as to the church's story is to take a walk around the church and the grounds and take in the nonverbal clues. Churches that are cluttered and in disrepair speak volumes about what is going on in the congregation and give hints about the stories being told. Use your senses and pay attention to not only what you see, but also what you smell and what you hear. Hoarding is a common phenomenon in congregations. A colleague described the congregational habit of "saving-everything-because-you-never-know-when-Sunday-school-curriculum-from-the 1940s-might-be-useful-again."[3] Hoarding, however, points to a story that involves living in the past, scarcity, and fear. Clutter and hoarding, along with being dirty and unkempt, also point to depression and low self-esteem within the congregation. To me, the physical evidence of the state of the building is one of the first clues of a history of clergy misconduct of some kind, usually sexual. Buildings that smell moldy say something profound about the story the congregational members tell themselves about who they are and what their sense of mission is all about. Congregations that keep their buildings up to date, clean, clutter-free, and attractive are more likely to be seen as warm and welcoming to visitors and potential members.

> Conflict can open the way for all the ghost stories of the past to come out. And until they do, they lie there festering and affecting the current life of the congregation.

Another way to find the clues to a congregation's story is to listen to what is being said about it in the community. Are people aware of the congregation? How is it perceived? Getting out into the surrounding community and asking around may reveal interesting information or it may tell you what you have suspected—they have no idea who it is. One of the scariest and most difficult questions I have ever asked congregations is, "If you were to no longer exist, what would be missed in this community?" The sad answer is too often, "We don't think anyone would notice." If what is being said about a congregation is a deafening silence, that is a tremendous clue about the story the congregational members are telling themselves: we are here for us. This extreme internal focus is slowly and assuredly killing many congregations.

On the other hand, one congregation I worked with struggled with a negative image in the community because of misinformation that was circulating. This congregation was known for having conflicts, and at one

Uncovering Clues to Your Church's Story

- Listen to how members talk about the church. What metaphors do they use? Do they express dreams and hopes? Fear and apprehension about the future? Do they refer to one moment as special or to a time when they were great?

- Poke around in the closets—both literal and figurative. What are the inglorious moments people want to hide? What sorts of stuff has been hidden away, out of sight?

- Take a walk around the church and the grounds. What do you see, smell, and hear? Is the building cluttered or dirty? Are the grounds well kept?

- Find out what is being said in the community. Are people aware of the congregation? How is it perceived? Ask the congregation, If we were to no longer exist, what would be missed in this community?

- Ask members to generate a list of words they think describe the congregation. What themes do you discover? What metaphors keep popping up? How imaginative are people in describing the congregation?

point their pastor had a heart attack and died, and his body was discovered on a Sunday morning. The rumor got out that he had committed suicide because the congregation was too difficult to deal with and their conflict and treatment of him had become more than he could bear. It was true the congregation was conflicted and there was a move afoot to have the pastor removed, but he did not commit suicide. Yet the larger community characterized this congregation and its conflicts as "the congregation that drove their pastor to commit suicide." This was quite the reputation and story to live down. It did bring members to the realization that they needed to address the conflicts in their midst and start sending a different message into the community.

A final way to look for clues to the story predominant in the congregation is to look in the mirror or hold up a figurative mirror to the congregation. Ask people to generate a list of words they think describe their congregation. What themes do you discover? What metaphors keep popping up? How imaginative are people in describing the congregation, or is everything pretty tried and true?

Putting all of these various clues together should allow observers to begin to paint a picture of who the church understands itself to be:

> "We are a family that loves our church and wants to enjoy each other's company."

> "We are a community of faith called by God to grow in faith and to be of service in the world."

> "We used to be a strong and thriving church, and now we are scared and on the verge of dying."

> "We are a justice-seeking congregation that is called to work for God's love, justice, and peace in the world."

These are simple stories, but they shape the understanding and future of a congregation. Conflict can be present in all of them, and change will be required to continue to live as a congregation, but the fearful church is less likely to weather either conflict or change well.

The stories congregations tell ourselves manifest in the issues we can't get past. One of the times stories begin to come out is during pastoral transition. One congregation I heard about in a meeting had been without a pastor for a significant period of time. A retired pastor confronted the denominational executive about the vacancy and asked when the judicatory leader was going to get the church a pastor. The executive's response stated that the congregation's members were in denial about who they were—a small, rural, declining congregation. The executive was clear that when they stopped thinking they were a big church that deserved a "traditional" pastor, meaning a man with a wife and children, and began to consider some of the fine pastors who would consider taking a call, he would help them. The story this congregation's members told themselves prevented them from considering any leadership they deemed not "pastoral material." The story was rooted in the congregation's past, not the reality of congregational life and leadership in the present moment.

Another congregation I worked with was wedded to the notion that they had to find a perfect pastor when the "perfect pastor" who had been serving them took another call. They spent almost three years hunting for a new pastor, turning down many viable and excellent candidates. Not long after they finally called someone, the pastor displayed behavior that indicated mental illness, which had been undiagnosed. The new pastor, in addition to being far from perfect, nearly destroyed the congregation in the eighteen months before the congregation fired the pastor. The next search was approached with great fear. The story moved from "the congregation wants a perfect pastor" to "the congregation is terrified of calling another bad pastor." A lot of work and coaching were required to rebuild confidence, set realistic expectations, and finally call a good, solid pastor. Success followed learning a new story.

Changing Your Story

Congregations can change our stories and reconceive who we are. We can go from seeing a dying, losing congregation to experiencing a new sense of mission and purpose. Making the shift all depends on the willingness to let go of old ideas and images and to discern what God is calling us to do in this time and place.

We have seen over the course of this book several congregations that changed their story and found new ways to be church. The church in a small town that decided that music was their new mission and the congregation that weathered botched conflict management and staff resignations before recapturing a mission-driven focus are but two examples. Each congregation that changes its story does so by coming to terms with the past, identifying the current story, locating itself within the larger narrative of biblical and Christian imagination, and dreaming and discerning a new future.

Healing Through Sermons

Congregations can use a variety of tools to come to terms with the past. Investigating the story is critical. Sermons related to the themes of the stories are an important follow-up. In the conflicted-and-chaotic to mission-driven congregation, the interim pastor used the story themes in a series of three sermons that came to be known as the "Come to Jesus" sermons. Each revealed different parts of the story and how that particular piece came to be part of the congregation's story. For instance, clergy sexual misconduct had occurred in the congregation's past, as mentioned above, and keeping secrets and denying any harm done in the congregation had become part of the story.

The secrecy and denial had created hidden emotions and tensions that had slowly festered over time and led to a mistrust of pastoral leadership, even though the current pastors had not done anything wrong. Newer pastors simply inherited the misplaced anger and shame warranted by much earlier colleagues. When the old secrets were revealed in the sermon, some people in the congregation were literally holding their breath, unable to believe that these secrets were being spoken aloud—and in worship, no less. The tension in the sanctuary was palpable. When the sermon was done, worshipers gave a collective sigh of relief, and after all three sermons were delivered, the metaphorical air in the church felt clearer and cleaner. The sermons were not easy to prepare, deliver, or hear, but they were necessary to the congregation's coming to grips with its past in order to be free to create a new story.

Building a Timeline

In addition to discovering the story and preaching about its themes, members of a congregation can benefit from revisiting our history. One tool for doing this is a visual timeline. Hang a horizontal strip of butcher paper around the walls of the fellowship hall or some other public and frequently travelled space in the church. On the butcher paper draw a horizontal line and mark off the decades of the congregation's life. Leave ample space for each decade and evenly divide the timeline among them. Mark the pastorates—fondly remembered or not.

Provide markers and sticky notes for members of the congregation to post on the timeline significant events in the life of the congregation. These can range from official moments, such as constructing the building or adding an education wing, to more personal events, such as the death of a matriarch or patriarch. Anything that any member regards as significant goes up on the timeline. No judgments. No commentary. No removal of sticky notes that contain something someone doesn't like. People should be invited to post the good, the bad, and even the ugly. Everything goes on the wall for everyone to see. And it is fine if people post the same thing more than once. This is not a voting process, but it does demonstrate that an event was important to multiple people. The timeline should remain up for at least a couple of weeks to allow people to make additions and to read it.

This exercise has several benefits. First, it allows everyone who wants to be involved to participate. So many times work on the congregation's goals, vision, and mission is delegated to a task force, and although people may get a chance to offer input, they rarely get a chance to participate in extended dialogue, mull over the discussion, and add more ideas to the process. The visual timeline invites contributions from those who have been members for a long time, newer members, and even younger members. Everyone's memories and significant events matter in creating the timeline. No opinion is differentiated or valued more than another.

Second, the exercise creates an openness to seeing what various members remember in the history and what they think was important. You may have to fill in the blanks in some of the earlier decades if no living members can add to those decades.

Third, the timeline offers everyone a fuller and nonthreatening look at the history of the congregation. Because the process does not allow for arguing over the events as posted and everyone has the right to add to the timeline from their own perspective, it becomes a witness to the whole congregation's thoughts and treats them with equanimity. Of course, leaders hope the timeline will provoke discussions, but there will be no debate about what is posted. It simply is what it is.

Plan for a discussion session or sessions after the timeline has been up for a while and everyone who wants to add to it has done so. The purpose of such gatherings is to give people an opportunity to discuss the themes that emerge in the information on the timeline. Begin the session with worship, and invite God to open everyone's eyes to see the wisdom revealed in the timeline. Invite people to walk around and review the information. Then invite them to break into small groups, and give them some simple focusing questions to begin discussion. Be sure to have small groups record their answers to the questions for sharing with the larger group. Here are some potential questions:

- Look at each decade of our congregation's history. What seem to be the predominant themes or patterns for each decade?
- Does the story of the congregation build toward the current time or do themes overlap between periods? If so, how? If the story dramatically changes, can you identify how and why it might have changed?
- Compare the themes and patterns between decades. Does history repeat itself? If so, how? Do some decades have themes that do not appear in others?

Groups might like to have an outside facilitator lead this discussion and give feedback afterward. Leaders could ask a small group from outside the congregation—people who are from other congregations or pastors or individuals from the mid-level judicatory of their denomination—to review the timeline and answer the discussion questions and then to compare their responses with those from your congregation's small-group discussions.

No matter what method you use to help a congregation come to terms with its history, the history is the starting point and helps you to identify the story operating within the congregation. This information allows you to move into the next phase of changing the story. But you can't change what you do not know. Discover the operating story!

Putting the Story in Context

Relating the congregation's story to the larger narratives of Scripture and Christian tradition is helpful. Congregations tend to feel we are alone and unique. There is something nice about being unique, but when coupled with the shame of being alone and thinking we are the only congregation that has ever struggled like this, the benefits of feeling unique cannot carry us through the struggle. Congregations need to understand we are part of something much larger—the wider church throughout time and around the world—and that membership includes sharing the struggles that have been experienced by the community of faith since the beginning.

An interesting exercise is to see what biblical story or stories a congregation relates to in our self-understanding. I have found that many congregations find comforting the fact that the majority of the letters in the Christian Scriptures were written to churches in conflict. We may not relate to the story of a particular church addressed in the letters, but we know that the early church was not idyllic and that we are not unfaithful for being in conflict. Even more powerful is for a congregation to find a positive model within the many stories of the Bible and Christian tradition to help us understand who we are. Equally informative would be the congregation's inability to relate to any biblical or historical narrative at all. This marks a lack of grounding in the traditions that are formative for a religious community. It calls

> We need to understand we are part of something much larger—the wider church throughout time and around the world—and we share the struggles that have been experienced by the community of faith since the beginning.

for another level of work to engage the congregation in discovering our roots and using those roots as a starting place for growth in the future.

The "Happy + Nice" congregation described earlier in this book found it related well to the various letters in the Christian Scriptures as members struggled to accept the conflict in their history, to assure themselves that they were not unfaithful, and at the same time to draw boundaries around ugly and unfaithful behavior of members during times of conflict. These early churches struggled in the same way. Their conflict and bad behavior and Paul's advice and theological framing helped the churches of his time, and centuries later inspired this congregation as it worked to turn itself around and move forward with mission and energy.

The small-town congregation that was slowly dwindling but found new energy by focusing on its gifts of music had explored passages regarding gifts and noticed that God gives different gifts to different people. They studied passages such as 1 Corinthians 12, where Paul teaches that God gives each person particular gifts for building up the body of Christ. The combination of believing that all have gifts and that all gifts are given by God is empowering to some congregations. The notion that one must use gifts for them truly to be received can also be motivating. Seeing itself as a gifted community put this congregation in a position to claim the gifts God had given it and to use those gifts wisely. Using those gifts then gave members energy to consider what else God might have given them that they could use for the benefit of others.

The congregation that went from flagship to troubled to thriving found companionship in both the prophetic writings of the Hebrew Bible and the stories of Jesus in the Gospels. The commands throughout the Hebrew Bible to care for the poor and the vulnerable, as well as the hospitality codes that instruct God's people to welcome the stranger, began to live in this congregation. Members took them seriously and began to look for ways to live those out in their ministries. Likewise, the teachings of Jesus to feed the hungry, clothe the naked, care for the outcast, and welcome the stranger were further evidence to this congregation of the call they felt from God to act on behalf of those who are marginalized in society. They discerned God's call to be a prophetic witness in the community and recognized that such a witness might bring them into conflict with the others in the wider community, just as the prophets angered political and religious leaders of their day and Jesus did in his day. The call to walk the path of Jesus, his ministry to the least and the outcast, inspired many of the ministries this church developed and continues to develop. Seeing the ancient stories live again in a contemporary context is a powerful witness.

Another congregation—when choosing to become more welcoming of lesbian, gay, bisexual, and transgender people—recalled stories from its own tradition about those who had in the past gone against the church and societal traditions because they felt called to offer a prophetic witness. The example of Dirk Willems cited in chapter 2 is inspirational in Anabaptist circles and beyond. The stories of early German evangelicals who established hospitals throughout the Midwest that treated people no matter their creed or race are also motivating. This open-door policy was risky at a time when people often discriminated based on religion or racial identity. The work of abolitionists from many different religious traditions to end slavery in the United States has also given inspiration to congregations.

As the congregation explored its tradition, stories began to emerge of brave forebearers who risked being shunned or losing their livelihood because they had stood against injustice in their time. These stories reminded this congregation that even though the current denominational leaders or the society around it didn't agree with its stand, members were not alone or unfaithful through their efforts. They were being exactly who they were, and their faithfulness was empowering.

Reflecting on Your Congregation . . .

1. What metaphors do people use to describe your congregation?

   What are the implications of those metaphors for your ability to change and address conflict?

2. What biblical stories or themes does your congregation feel the most affinity to?

   Why are those stories or themes important in the life of your congregation?

3. What themes can you identify in your congregation's current story?

   What do those themes say about the future of your congregation?

4. What tools discussed in this chapter would help your congregation begin to change its story?

Benediction

For a congregation to know we are not alone, that others have travelled this road before, that we are being faithful by struggling, and that we stand on broad shoulders, even as we do a new thing, is helpful, inspiring, and comforting. For a congregation to free our imagination, dream, and discern a new future that answers God's call to mission and ministry is vital. The church was never meant to be internally focused, whether adrift from the traditions or wed to them.

When a congregation can move forward from conflict, weather change well, and move beyond our old and outdated stories, we are able to create a new story for our future. The question is not "What do we have to settle for?" but rather "With God's help, how good do we want our life to be as a congregation?"

Do we dare to dream into the future? Do we dare to ask God to lead us to a new place? Do we dare, in some cases, to ask God if these dry and old bones can live? The future is wide open with God, if we dare.

Notes

Introduction

1. See Anita L. Bradshaw, "Leadership Theory from 1900 to the Present" (unpublished paper, Luther Seminary, 2001); Anita L. Bradshaw, "Theological Perspectives for an Integrated Theory" (unpublished paper, Luther Seminary, 2001).

Chapter One

1. A large body of literature addresses this reality. Works by Diana Butler Bass, Phyllis Tickle, the Gospel and Our Culture Network, the missional church movement, the emergent church movement, and many others have addressed these issues, and many congregations and leaders have learned from them.

Chapter Two

1. David E. Fredrickson, *Eros and the Christ: Longing and Envy in Paul's Christology* (Minneapolis: Fortress Press, 2013), 106.

2. N. T. Wright, *Paul for Everyone: 2 Corinthians* (London: SPCK, 2003; London: SPCK / Louisville: Westminster John Knox Press, 2004), 65.

3. Diana Butler Bass, *A People's History of Christianity: The Other Side of the Story* (New York: HarperCollins, 2009), 6.

4. Lesley Poling-Kempes, *Ghost Ranch* (Tucson: University of Arizona Press, 2005), 232.

5. I have been unable to find a source for this quote and it seems, therefore, to be a paraphrase. Perhaps it is not Moltmann, but it is in keeping with much of his writing on the Holy Spirit.

Chapter Three

1. Michael Gryboski, "PCUSA Decline in Churches, Members Continued in 2013," *Christian Post*, June 2, 2014, www.christianpost.com/news/pcusa-decline-in-churches-members-continued-in-2013-120725/.

2. "U.S. Religious Landscape Survey: Religious Affiliation," Pew Research Religion and Public Life Project, February 1, 2008, www.pewforum.org/2008/02/01/u-s-religious-landscape-survey-religious-affiliation/.

3. "Study: 'I Know What You Did Last Sunday' Finds Americans Significantly Inflate Religious Participation," Public Religion Research Institute, May 17, 2014, http://publicreligion.org/research/2014/05/aapor-2014/.

4. Everett M. Rogers, *Diffusion of Innovations* (New York: Free Press, 1995), 163.

5. Ibid., 262.

6. Ronald A. Heifetz, Alexander Grashow, and Marty Linsky, *The Practice of Adaptive Leadership: Tools and Tactics for Changing Your Organization and the World* (Boston: Harvard Business Press, 2009), 16.

7. Ibid., 14.

Chapter Four

1. Speed B. Leas, *Moving Your Church Through Conflict* (Lanham, MD: Rowman and Littlefield, 1985), 19.

2. Ibid.

3. Ibid., 22.

4. Ibid.

5. Ibid.

6. I learned this technique, called "Dwelling in the Word," from the church-renewal organization Church Innovations. More information can be found at www.churchinnovations.org/06_about/dwelling.html.

7. Nancy L. Bieber, *Decision Making and Spiritual Discernment: The Sacred Art of Finding Your Way* (Woodstock, VT: SkyLight Paths, 2010), 6.

8. Ibid., 7.

9. Diane M. Millis, *Conversation—The Sacred Art: Practicing Presence in an Age of Distraction* (Woodstock, VT: SkyLight Paths, 2013), xv.

10. Adapted from "Guidelines for Healthy Communications," Mayflower Community Congregational Church, United Church of Christ, Minneapolis, Minnesota, www.mayflowermpls.org/our-life-together/68.

Chapter Five

1. The Center for Progressive Renewal, "What Is a Next Level Church?" http://progressiverenewal.org/revitalize-your-church/nextlevel/. Accessed December 17, 2014. Graph used by permission.

2. See Luther K. Snow, *The Power of Asset Mapping: How Your Congregation Can Act on Its Gifts* (Lanham, MD: Rowman and Littlefield, 2004).

3. Snow, *The Power of Asset Mapping*, 15–20. The entire process is summarized in this section of the book.

4. Roy M. Oswald and Barry Johnson, *Managing Polarities in Congregations: Eight Keys for Thriving Faith Communities* (Lanham, MD: Rowman and Littlefield Publishers, 2009), 4–5.

5. Barry Johnson, *Polarity Management: Identifying and Managing Unsolvable Problems* (Amherst, MA: HRD Press, 2014), 106.

Chapter Six

1. Larry A. Golemon, ed., *Living Our Story: Narrative Leadership and Congregational Culture*, Narrative Leadership Collection (Lanham, MD: Rowman and Littlefield, 2010), 3.

2. Diana Butler Bass, "Living Our Story," *Leadership in Congregations*, ed. Richard Bass (Lanham, MD: Rowman and Littlefield, 2006), xi.

3. Derek Penwell, "Why Trashing Jesus Is the Right Thing to Do," *[D]mergent* (blog), September 8, 2014, http://dmergent.org/articles/2012/9/22/trashing-jesus-a-social-media-rorschach-test.

Suggested Resources

Bieber, Nancy L. *Decision Making and Spiritual Discernment: The Sacred Art of Finding Your Way*. Woodstock, VT: SkyLight Paths, 2010.

Butler Bass, Diana. *Christianity After Religion: The End of Church and the Birth of a New Spiritual Awakening*. New York: HarperOne, 2012.

———. *A People's History of Christianity: The Other Side of the Story*. New York: HarperCollins, 2009.

Golemon, Larry A., ed. *Finding Our Story: Narrative Leadership and Congregational Change*. Lanham, MD: Rowman and Littlefield, 2010.

———. *Living Our Story: Narrative Leadership and Congregational Culture*. Lanham, MD: Rowman and Littlefield, 2010.

———. *Teaching Our Story: Narrative Leadership and Pastoral Formation*. Lanham, MD: Rowman and Littlefield, 2010.

Heifetz, Ronald A., Alexander Grashow, and Marty Linsky. *The Practice of Adaptive Leadership: Tools and Tactics for Changing Your Organization and the World*. Boston: Harvard Business Press, 2009.

Johnson, Barry. *Polarity Management: Identifying and Managing Unsolvable Problems*. Amherst, MA: HRD Press, 2014.

Johnson, Luke Timothy. *Scripture and Discernment: Decision Making in the Church*. Nashville: Abingdon, 1996.

Kraybill, Ronald S. *Repairing the Breach: Ministering in Community Conflict*. Scottdale, PA: Herald Press, 1981.

Leas, Speed B. *Moving Your Church Through Conflict*. Lanham, MD: Rowman and Littlefield, 1985.

Lederach, John Paul. *The Journey Toward Reconciliation*. Scottdale, PA: Herald Press, 1999.

Lott, David B., ed. *Conflict Management in Congregations*. Lanham, MD: Rowman and Littlefield, 2001.

Millis, Diane M. *Conversation—The Sacred Art: Practicing Presence in an Age of Distraction*. Woodstock, VT: SkyLight Paths, 2013.

Oswald, Roy M., and Barry Johnson. *Managing Polarities in Congregations: Eight Keys for Thriving Faith Communities*. Lanham, MD: Rowman and Littlefield, 2009.

Piazza, Michael S., and Cameron B. Trimble. *Liberating Hope! Daring to Renew the Mainline Church.* Cleveland: Pilgrim Press, 2011.

Rogers, Everett M. *Diffusion of Innovations.* 5th ed. New York: Free Press, 2005.

Snow, Luther K. *The Power of Asset Mapping: How Your Congregation Can Act on Its Gifts.* Lanham, MD: Rowman and Littlefield, 2004.

Tickle, Phyllis. *The Great Emergence: How Christianity Is Changing and Why.* Grand Rapids, MI: Baker Books, 2012.

Inspiration

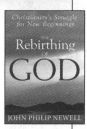

The Rebirthing of God
Christianity's Struggle for New Beginnings
By John Philip Newell
Drawing on modern prophets from East and West, and using the holy island of Iona as an icon of new beginnings, Celtic poet, peacemaker and scholar John Philip Newell dares us to imagine a new birth from deep within Christianity, a fresh stirring of the Spirit.
6 x 9, 160 pp, HC, 978-1-59473-542-4 **$19.99**

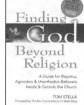

Finding God Beyond Religion: A Guide for Skeptics, Agnostics & Unorthodox Believers Inside & Outside the Church
By Tom Stella; Foreword by The Rev. Canon Marianne Wells Borg
Reinterprets traditional religious teachings central to the Christian faith for people who have outgrown the beliefs and devotional practices that once made sense to them.
6 x 9, 160 pp, Quality PB, 978-1-59473-485-4 **$16.99**

Fully Awake and Truly Alive: Spiritual Practices to Nurture Your Soul
By Rev. Jane E. Vennard; Foreword by Rami Shapiro
Illustrates the joys and frustrations of spiritual practice, offers insights from various religious traditions and provides exercises and meditations to help us become more fully alive.
6 x 9, 208 pp, Quality PB, 978-1-59473-473-1 **$16.99**

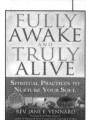

Journeys of Simplicity: Traveling Light with Thomas Merton, Bashō, Edward Abbey, Annie Dillard & Others *By Philip Harnden*
Invites you to consider a more graceful way of traveling through life. Includes journal pages to help you get started on your own spiritual journey.
5 x 7¼, 144 pp, Quality PB, 978-1-59473-181-5 **$12.99**

Perennial Wisdom for the Spiritually Independent
Sacred Teachings—Annotated & Explained
Annotation by Rami Shapiro; Foreword by Richard Rohr
Weaves sacred texts and teachings from the world's major religions into a coherent exploration of the five core questions at the heart of every religion's search.
5½ x 8½, 336 pp, Quality PB, 978-1-59473-515-8 **$16.99**

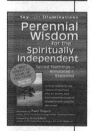

Saving Civility: 52 Ways to Tame Rude, Crude & Attitude for a Polite Planet
By Sara Hacala
Provides fifty-two practical ways you can reverse the course of incivility and make the world a more enriching, pleasant place to live.
6 x 9, 240 pp, Quality PB, 978-1-59473-314-7 **$16.99**

Spiritually Healthy Divorce: Navigating Disruption with Insight & Hope
By Carolyne Call
A spiritual map to help you move through the twists and turns of divorce.
6 x 9, 224 pp, Quality PB, 978-1-59473-288-1 **$16.99**

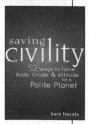

Sacred Texts—SkyLight Illuminations Series

Offers today's spiritual seeker an enjoyable entry into the great classic texts of the world's spiritual traditions. Each classic is presented in an accessible translation, with facing pages of guided commentary from experts, giving you the keys you need to understand the history, context and meaning of the text.

CHRISTIANITY

The Book of Common Prayer: A Spiritual Treasure Chest—Selections Annotated & Explained
Annotation by The Rev. Canon C. K. Robertson, PhD; Foreword by The Most Rev. Katharine Jefferts Schori; Preface by Archbishop Desmond Tutu
Makes available the riches of this spiritual treasure chest for all who are interested in deepening their life of prayer, building stronger relationships and making a difference in their world. 5½ x 8½, 208 pp, Quality PB, 978-1-59473-524-0 **$16.99**

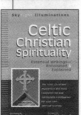

Celtic Christian Spirituality: Essential Writings—Annotated & Explained
Annotation by Mary C. Earle; Foreword by John Philip Newell
Explores how the writings of this lively tradition embody the gospel.
5½ x 8½, 176 pp, Quality PB, 978-1-59473-302-4 **$16.99**

Desert Fathers and Mothers: Early Christian Wisdom Sayings—Annotated & Explained *Annotation by Christine Valters Paintner, PhD*
Opens up wisdom of the desert fathers and mothers for readers with no previous knowledge of Western monasticism and early Christianity.
5½ x 8½, 192 pp, Quality PB, 978-1-59473-373-4 **$16.99**

The End of Days: Essential Selections from Apocalyptic Texts—Annotated & Explained *Annotation by Robert G. Clouse, PhD*
Helps you understand the complex Christian visions of the end of the world.
5½ x 8½, 224 pp, Quality PB, 978-1-59473-170-9 **$16.99**

The Hidden Gospel of Matthew: Annotated & Explained
Translation & Annotation by Ron Miller
Discover the words and events that have the strongest connection to the historical Jesus.
5½ x 8½, 272 pp, Quality PB, 978-1-59473-038-2 **$16.99**

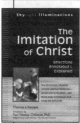

The Imitation of Christ: Selections Annotated & Explained
Annotation by Paul Wesley Chilcote, PhD; By Thomas à Kempis; Adapted from John Wesley's The Christian's Pattern
Let Jesus's example of holiness, humility and purity of heart be a companion on your own spiritual journey.
5½ x 8½, 224 pp, Quality PB, 978-1-59473-434-2 **$16.99**

The Infancy Gospels of Jesus: Apocryphal Tales from the Childhoods of Mary and Jesus—Annotated & Explained
Translation & Annotation by Stevan Davies; Foreword by A. Edward Siecienski, PhD
A startling presentation of the early lives of Mary, Jesus and other biblical figures that will amuse and surprise you. 5½ x 8½, 176 pp, Quality PB, 978-1-59473-258-4 **$16.99**

John & Charles Wesley: Selections from Their Writings and Hymns—Annotated & Explained *Annotation by Paul W. Chilcote, PhD*
A unique presentation of the writings of these two inspiring brothers brings together some of the most essential material from their large corpus of work.
5½ x 8½, 288 pp, Quality PB, 978-1-59473-309-3 **$16.99**

Julian of Norwich: Selections from *Revelations of Divine Love*—Annotated & Explained *Annotation by Mary C. Earle; Foreword by Roberta C. Bondi*
Addresses topics including the infinite nature of God, the life of prayer, God's suffering with us, the eternal and undying life of the soul, the motherhood of Jesus and the motherhood of God and more.
5½ x 8½, 224 pp, Quality PB, 978-1-59473-513-4 **$16.99**

Sacred Texts—continued

CHRISTIANITY—continued

The Lost Sayings of Jesus: Teachings from Ancient Christian, Jewish, Gnostic and Islamic Sources—Annotated & Explained
Translation & Annotation by Andrew Phillip Smith; Foreword by Stephan A. Hoeller
Depicts Jesus as a Wisdom teacher who speaks to people of all faiths as a mystic and spiritual master. 5½ x 8½, 240 pp, Quality PB, 978-1-59473-172-3 **$16.99**

Philokalia: The Eastern Christian Spiritual Texts—Selections
Annotated & Explained *Annotation by Allyne Smith; Translation by G. E. H. Palmer, Phillip Sherrard and Bishop Kallistos Ware* The first approachable introduction to the wisdom of the Philokalia. 5½ x 8½, 240 pp, Quality PB, 978-1-59473-103-7 **$18.99**

The Sacred Writings of Paul: Selections Annotated & Explained
Translation & Annotation by Ron Miller Leads you into the exciting immediacy of Paul's teachings. 5½ x 8½, 224 pp, Quality PB, 978-1-59473-213-3 **$16.99**

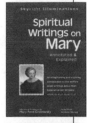

Saint Augustine of Hippo: Selections from *Confessions* and Other Essential Writings—Annotated & Explained
Annotation by Joseph T. Kelley, PhD; Translation by the Augustinian Heritage Institute
Provides insight into the mind and heart of this foundational Christian figure.
5½ x 8½, 272 pp, Quality PB, 978-1-59473-282-9 **$16.99**

Saint Ignatius Loyola—The Spiritual Writings: Selections
Annotated & Explained *Annotation by Mark Mossa, SJ* Focuses on the practical mysticism of Ignatius of Loyola. 5½ x 8½, 288 pp, Quality PB, 978-1-59473-301-7 **$18.99**

Sex Texts from the Bible: Selections Annotated & Explained
Translation & Annotation by Teresa J. Hornsby; Foreword by Amy-Jill Levine
Demystifies the Bible's ideas on gender roles, marriage, sexual orientation, virginity, lust and sexual pleasure. 5½ x 8½, 208 pp, Quality PB, 978-1-59473-217-1 **$16.99**

Spiritual Writings on Mary: Annotated & Explained
Annotation by Mary Ford-Grabowsky; Foreword by Andrew Harvey
Examines the role of Mary, the mother of Jesus, as a source of inspiration in history and in life today. 5½ x 8½, 272 pp, Quality PB, 978-1-59473-001-6 **$16.99**

The Way of a Pilgrim: The Jesus Prayer Journey—Annotated & Explained
Translation & Annotation by Gleb Pokrovsky; Foreword by Andrew Harvey A classic of Russian Orthodox spirituality. 5½ x 8½, 160 pp, Illus., Quality PB, 978-1-893361-31-7 **$15.99**

GNOSTICISM

Gnostic Writings on the Soul: Annotated & Explained
Translation & Annotation by Andrew Phillip Smith; Foreword by Stephan A. Hoeller
Reveals the inspiring ways your soul can remember and return to its unique, divine purpose. 5½ x 8½, 144 pp, Quality PB, 978-1-59473-220-1 **$16.99**

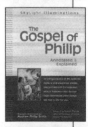

The Gospel of Philip: Annotated & Explained
Translation & Annotation by Andrew Phillip Smith; Foreword by Stevan Davies
Reveals otherwise unrecorded sayings of Jesus and fragments of Gnostic mythology.
5½ x 8½, 160 pp, Quality PB, 978-1-59473-111-2 **$16.99**

The Gospel of Thomas: Annotated & Explained
Translation & Annotation by Stevan Davies; Foreword by Andrew Harvey
Sheds new light on the origins of Christianity and portrays Jesus as a wisdom-loving sage.
5½ x 8½, 192 pp, Quality PB, 978-1-893361-45-4 **$16.99**

The Secret Book of John: The Gnostic Gospel—Annotated & Explained
Translation & Annotation by Stevan Davies The most significant and influential text of the ancient Gnostic religion. 5½ x 8½, 208 pp, Quality PB, 978-1-59473-082-5 **$18.99**

See Inspiration for *Perennial Wisdom for the Spiritually Independent: Sacred Teachings—Annotated & Explained*

Spirituality

The Forgiveness Handbook
Spiritual Wisdom and Practice for the Journey to Freedom, Healing and Peace
Created by the Editors at SkyLight Paths; Introduction by The Rev. Canon Marianne Wells Borg
Offers inspiration, encouragement and spiritual practice from across faith traditions for all who seek hope, wholeness and the freedom that comes from true forgiveness.
6 x 9, 256 pp, Quality PB, 978-1-59473-577-6 **$18.99**

Like a Child
Restoring the Awe, Wonder, Joy and Resiliency of the Human Spirit
By Rev. Timothy J. Mooney

By breaking free from our misperceptions about what it means to be an adult, we can reshape our world and become harbingers of grace. This unique spiritual resource explores Jesus's counsel to become like children in order to enter the kingdom of God. 6 x 9, 160 pp, Quality PB, 978-1-59473-543-1 **$16.99**

The Passionate Jesus: What We Can Learn from Jesus about Love, Fear, Grief, Joy and Living Authentically
By The Rev. Peter Wallace
Reveals Jesus as a passionate figure who was involved, present, connected, honest and direct with others and encourages you to build personal authenticity in every area of your own life. 6 x 9, 208 pp, Quality PB, 978-1-59473-393-2 **$18.99**

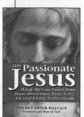

Gathering at God's Table: The Meaning of Mission in the Feast of Faith
By Katharine Jefferts Schori
A profound reminder of our role in the larger frame of God's dream for a restored and reconciled world. 6 x 9, 256 pp, HC, 978-1-59473-316-1 **$21.99**

The Heartbeat of God: Finding the Sacred in the Middle of Everything
By Katharine Jefferts Schori; Foreword by Joan Chittister, OSB
Explores our connections to other people, to other nations and with the environment through the lens of faith.
6 x 9, 240 pp, HC, 978-1-59473-292-8 **$21.99**; Quality PB, 978-1-59473-589-9 **$16.99**

A Dangerous Dozen: Twelve Christians Who Threatened the Status Quo but Taught Us to Live Like Jesus
By The Rev. Canon C. K. Robertson, PhD; Foreword by Archbishop Desmond Tutu
Profiles twelve visionary men and women who challenged society and showed the world a different way of living.
6 x 9, 208 pp, Quality PB, 978-1-59473-298-0 **$16.99**

Laugh Your Way to Grace: Reclaiming the Spiritual Power of Humor
By Rev. Susan Sparks
A powerful, humorous case for laughter as a spiritual, healing path.
6 x 9, 176 pp, Quality PB, 978-1-59473-280-5 **$16.99**

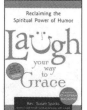

Claiming Earth as Common Ground: The Ecological Crisis through the Lens of Faith
By Andrea Cohen-Kiener; Foreword by Rev. Sally Bingham
6 x 9, 192 pp, Quality PB, 978-1-59473-261-4 **$16.99**

Living into Hope: A Call to Spiritual Action for Such a Time as This
By Rev. Dr. Joan Brown Campbell; Foreword by Karen Armstrong
6 x 9, 208 pp, Quality PB, 978-1-59473-436-6 **$18.99**; HC, 978-1-59473-283-6 **$21.99**

Renewal in the Wilderness
A Spiritual Guide to Connecting with God in the Natural World
By John Lionberger 6 x 9, 176 pp, b/w photos, Quality PB, 978-1-59473-219-5 **$16.99**

Spiritual Adventures in the Snow
Skiing & Snowboarding as Renewal for Your Soul
By Dr. Marcia McFee and Rev. Karen Foster; Foreword by Paul Arthur
5½ x 8½, 208 pp, Quality PB, 978-1-59473-270-6 **$16.99**

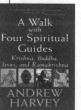

A Walk with Four Spiritual Guides: Krishna, Buddha, Jesus, and Ramakrishna
By Andrew Harvey 5½ x 8½, 192 pp, b/w photos & illus., Quality PB, 978-1-59473-138-9 **$15.99**

Spirituality / Animal Companions

Blessing the Animals
Prayers and Ceremonies to Celebrate God's Creatures, Wild and Tame
Edited and with Introductions by Lynn L. Caruso
5 x 7¼, 256 pp, Quality PB, 978-1-59473-253-9 **$15.99**; HC, 978-1-59473-145-7 **$19.99**

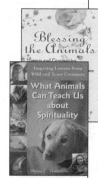

Remembering My Pet
A Kid's Own Spiritual Workbook for When a Pet Dies
By Nechama Liss-Levinson, PhD, and Rev. Molly Phinney Baskette, MDiv
Foreword by Lynn L. Caruso
8 x 10, 48 pp, 2-color text, HC, 978-1-59473-221-8 **$16.99**

What Animals Can Teach Us about Spirituality
Inspiring Lessons from Wild and Tame Creatures
By Diana L. Guerrero 6 x 9, 176 pp, Quality PB, 978-1-893361-84-3 **$18.99**

Spirituality & Crafts

Beading—The Creative Spirit
Finding Your Sacred Center through the Art of Beadwork
By Rev. Wendy Ellsworth
Invites you on a spiritual pilgrimage into the kaleidoscope world of glass and color.
7 x 9, 240 pp, 8-page color insert, 40+ b/w photos and 40 diagrams
Quality PB, 978-1-59473-267-6 **$18.99**

Contemplative Crochet
A Hands-On Guide for Interlocking Faith and Craft
By Cindy Crandall-Frazier; Foreword by Linda Skolnik
Illuminates the spiritual lessons you can learn through crocheting.
7 x 9, 208 pp, b/w photos, Quality PB, 978-1-59473-238-6 **$16.99**

The Knitting Way
A Guide to Spiritual Self-Discovery
By Linda Skolnik and Janice MacDaniels
Examines how you can explore and strengthen your spiritual life through knitting.
7 x 9, 240 pp, b/w photos, Quality PB, 978-1-59473-079-5 **$16.99**

The Painting Path
Embodying Spiritual Discovery through Yoga, Brush and Color
By Linda Novick; Foreword by Richard Segalman
Explores the divine connection you can experience through art.
7 x 9, 208 pp, 8-page color insert, plus b/w photos, Quality PB, 978-1-59473-226-3 **$18.99**

The Quilting Path
A Guide to Spiritual Discovery through Fabric, Thread and Kabbalah
By Louise Silk
Explores how to cultivate personal growth through quilt making.
7 x 9, 192 pp, b/w photos and illus., Quality PB, 978-1-59473-206-5 **$16.99**

The Scrapbooking Journey
A Hands-On Guide to Spiritual Discovery
By Cory Richardson-Lauve; Foreword by Stacy Julian
Reveals how this craft can become a practice used to deepen and shape your life.
7 x 9, 176 pp, 8-page color insert, plus b/w photos, Quality PB, 978-1-59473-216-4 **$18.99**

The Soulwork of Clay
A Hands-On Approach to Spirituality
By Marjory Zoet Bankson; Photos by Peter Bankson
Takes you through the seven-step process of making clay into a pot, drawing
parallels at each stage to the process of spiritual growth.
7 x 9, 192 pp, b/w photos, Quality PB, 978-1-59473-249-2 **$16.99**

Spiritual Practice—The Sacred Art of Living Series

Dreaming—The Sacred Art: Incubating, Navigating & Interpreting Sacred Dreams for Spiritual & Personal Growth
By Lori Joan Swick, PhD
This fascinating introduction to sacred dreams celebrates the dream experience as a way to deepen spiritual awareness and as a source of self-healing. Designed for the novice and the experienced sacred dreamer of all faith traditions, or none.
5½ x 8½, 224 pp, Quality PB, 978-1-59473-544-8 **$16.99**

Conversation—The Sacred Art: Practicing Presence in an Age of Distraction
By Diane M. Millis, PhD; Foreword by Rev. Tilden Edwards, PhD
5½ x 8½, 192 pp, Quality PB, 978-1-59473-474-8 **$16.99**

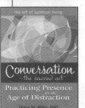

Dance—The Sacred Art: The Joy of Movement as a Spiritual Practice
By Cynthia Winton-Henry 5½ x 8½, 224 pp, Quality PB, 978-1-59473-268-3 **$16.99**

Fly-Fishing—The Sacred Art: Casting a Fly as a Spiritual Practice
By Rabbi Eric Eisenkramer and Rev. Michael Attas, MD; Foreword by Chris Wood, CEO, Trout Unlimited; Preface by Lori Simon, executive director, Casting for Recovery
5½ x 8½, 160 pp, Quality PB, 978-1-59473-299-7 **$16.99**

Giving—The Sacred Art: Creating a Lifestyle of Generosity
By Lauren Tyler Wright 5½ x 8½, 208 pp, Quality PB, 978-1-59473-224-9 **$16.99**

Haiku—The Sacred Art: A Spiritual Practice in Three Lines
By Margaret D. McGee 5½ x 8½, 192 pp, Quality PB, 978-1-59473-269-0 **$16.99**

Hospitality—The Sacred Art: Discovering the Hidden Spiritual Power of Invitation and Welcome *By Rev. Nanette Sawyer; Foreword by Rev. Dirk Ficca*
5½ x 8½, 208 pp, Quality PB, 978-1-59473-228-7 **$16.99**

Labyrinths from the Outside In, 2nd Edition
Walking to Spiritual Insight—A Beginner's Guide *By Rev. Dr. Donna Schaper and Rev. Dr. Carole Ann Camp* 6 x 9, 208 pp, b/w illus. and photos, Quality PB, 978-1-59473-486-1 **$16.99**

Lectio Divina—**The Sacred Art**
Transforming Words & Images into Heart-Centered Prayer
By Christine Valters Paintner, PhD 5½ x 8½, 240 pp, Quality PB, 978-1-59473-300-0 **$16.99**

Pilgrimage—The Sacred Art: Journey to the Center of the Heart
By Dr. Sheryl A. Kujawa-Holbrook 5½ x 8½, 240 pp, Quality PB, 978-1-59473-472-4 **$16.99**

Practicing the Sacred Art of Listening
A Guide to Enrich Your Relationships and Kindle Your Spiritual Life
By Kay Lindahl 8 x 8, 176 pp, Quality PB, 978-1-893361-85-0 **$18.99**

Recovery—The Sacred Art: The Twelve Steps as Spiritual Practice *By Rami Shapiro*
Foreword by Joan Borysenko, PhD 5½ x 8½, 240 pp, Quality PB, 978-1-59473-259-1 **$16.99**

Running—The Sacred Art: Preparing to Practice *By Dr. Warren A. Kay*
Foreword by Kristin Armstrong 5½ x 8½, 160 pp, Quality PB, 978-1-59473-227-0 **$16.99**

The Sacred Art of Chant: Preparing to Practice
By Ana Hernández 5½ x 8½, 192 pp, Quality PB, 978-1-59473-036-8 **$16.99**

The Sacred Art of Fasting: Preparing to Practice
By Thomas Ryan, CSP 5½ x 8½, 192 pp, Quality PB, 978-1-59473-078-8 **$15.99**

The Sacred Art of Forgiveness: Forgiving Ourselves and Others through God's Grace
By Marcia Ford 8 x 8, 176 pp, Quality PB, 978-1-59473-175-4 **$18.99**

The Sacred Art of Listening: Forty Reflections for Cultivating a Spiritual Practice
By Kay Lindahl; Illus. by Amy Schnapper 8 x 8, 160 pp, b/w illus., Quality PB, 978-1-893361-44-7 **$16.99**

The Sacred Art of Lovingkindness: Preparing to Practice
By Rabbi Rami Shapiro; Foreword by Marcia Ford 5½ x 8½, 176 pp, Quality PB, 978-1-59473-151-8 **$16.99**

Thanking & Blessing—The Sacred Art: Spiritual Vitality through Gratefulness
By Jay Marshall, PhD; Foreword by Philip Gulley 5½ x 8½, 176 pp, Quality PB, 978-1-59473-231-7 **$16.99**

Writing—The Sacred Art: Beyond the Page to Spiritual Practice
By Rami Shapiro and Aaron Shapiro 5½ x 8½, 192 pp, Quality PB, 978-1-59473-372-7 **$16.99**

Prayer / Meditation

Calling on God
Inclusive Christian Prayers for Three Years of Sundays
By Peter Bankson and Deborah Sokolove
Prayers for today's world, vividly written for Christians who long for a way to talk to and about God that feels fresh yet still connected to tradition.
6 x 9, 400 pp, Quality PB, 978-1-59473-568-4 **$18.99**

Openings, 2nd Edition
A Daybook of Saints, Sages, Psalms and Prayer Practices
By Rev. Larry J. Peacock
For anyone hungry for a richer prayer life, this prayer book offers daily inspiration to help you move closer to God. Draws on a wide variety of resources—lives of saints and sages from every age, psalms, and suggestions for personal reflection and practice. 6 x 9, 448 pp, Quality PB, 978-1-59473-545-5 **$18.99**

Men Pray: Voices of Strength, Faith, Healing, Hope and Courage
Created by the Editors at SkyLight Paths; With Introductions by Brian D. McLaren
Celebrates the rich variety of ways men around the world have called out to the Divine—with words of joy, praise, gratitude, wonder, petition and even anger—from the ancient world up to our own day.
5 x 7¼, 192 pp, HC, 978-1-59473-395-6 **$16.99**

Honest to God Prayer: Spirituality as Awareness, Empowerment,
Relinquishment and Paradox *By Kent Ira Groff*
6 x 9, 192 pp, Quality PB, 978-1-59473-433-5 **$16.99**

Lectio Divina—The Sacred Art
Transforming Words & Images into Heart-Centered Prayer
By Christine Valters Paintner, PhD
5½ x 8½, 240 pp, Quality PB, 978-1-59473-300-0 **$16.99**

Sacred Attention: A Spiritual Practice for Finding God in the Moment
By Margaret D. McGee
6 x 9, 144 pp, Quality PB, 978-1-59473-291-1 **$16.99**

Secrets of Prayer: A Multifaith Guide to Creating Personal Prayer in Your Life
By Nancy Corcoran, CSJ
6 x 9, 160 pp, Quality PB, 978-1-59473-215-7 **$16.99**

Women of Color Pray: Voices of Strength, Faith, Healing, Hope and Courage
Edited and with Introductions by Christal M. Jackson
5 x 7¼, 208 pp, Quality PB, 978-1-59473-077-1 **$15.99**

Prayer / M. Basil Pennington, OCSO

Finding Grace at the Center, 3rd Edition: The Beginning of
Centering Prayer *With Thomas Keating, OCSO, and Thomas E. Clarke, SJ*
Foreword by Rev. Cynthia Bourgeault, PhD A practical guide to a simple and beautiful form of meditative prayer. 5 x 7¼, 128 pp, Quality PB, 978-1-59473-182-2 **$12.99**

The Monks of Mount Athos: A Western Monk's Extraordinary
Spiritual Journey on Eastern Holy Ground *Foreword by Archimandrite Dionysios*
Explores the landscape, monastic communities and food of Athos.
6 x 9, 352 pp, Quality PB, 978-1-893361-78-2 **$18.95**

Psalms: A Spiritual Commentary *Illus. by Phillip Ratner*
Reflections on some of the most beloved passages from the Bible's most widely read book. 6 x 9, 176 pp, 24 full-page b/w illus., Quality PB, 978-1-59473-234-8 **$16.99**

The Song of Songs: A Spiritual Commentary *Illus. by Phillip Ratner*
Explore the Bible's most challenging mystical text.
6 x 9, 160 pp, 14 full-page b/w illus., Quality PB, 978-1-59473-235-5 **$16.99**
HC, 978-1-59473-004-7 **$19.99**

Retirement and Later-Life Spirituality

Caresharing
A Reciprocal Approach to Caregiving and Care Receiving in the Complexities of Aging, Illness or Disability
By Marty Richards
Shows how to move from independent to *inter*dependent caregiving, so that the "cared for" and the "carer" share a deep sense of connection.
6 x 9, 256 pp, Quality PB, 978-1-59473-286-7 **$16.99**; HC, 978-1-59473-247-8 **$24.99**

How Did I Get to Be 70 When I'm 35 Inside?
Spiritual Surprises of Later Life
By Linda Douty
Encourages you to focus on the inner changes of aging to help you greet your later years as the grand adventure they can be.
6 x 9, 208 pp, Quality PB, 978-1-59473-297-3 **$16.99**

Soul Fire
Accessing Your Creativity
By Thomas Ryan, CSP
This inspiring guide shows you how to cultivate your creative spirit, particularly in the second half of life, as a way to encourage personal growth, enrich your spiritual life and deepen your communion with God.
6 x 9, 160 pp, Quality PB, 978-1-59473-243-0 **$16.99**

Restoring Life's Missing Pieces
The Spiritual Power of Remembering & Reuniting with People, Places, Things & Self
By Caren Goldman; Foreword by Dr. Nancy Copeland-Payton
Delve deeply into ways that your body, mind and spirit answer the Spirit of Re-union's calls to reconnect with people, places, things and self. A powerful and thought-provoking look at "reunions" of all kinds as roads to remembering the missing pieces of our stories, psyches and souls.
6 x 9, 208 pp, Quality PB, 978-1-59473-295-9 **$16.99**

Creative Aging
Rethinking Retirement and Non-Retirement in a Changing World
By Marjory Zoet Bankson
Explores the spiritual dimensions of retirement and aging and offers creative ways for you to share your gifts and experience, particularly when retirement leaves you questioning who you are when you are no longer defined by your career.
6 x 9, 160 pp, Quality PB, 978-1-59473-281-2 **$16.99**

Creating a Spiritual Retirement
A Guide to the Unseen Possibilities in Our Lives
By Molly Srode
Retirement can be an opportunity to refocus on your soul and deepen the presence of spirit in your life. With fresh spiritual reflections and questions to help you explore this new phase.
6 x 9, 208 pp, b/w photos, Quality PB, 978-1-59473-050-4 **$14.99**

Keeping Spiritual Balance as We Grow Older
More than 65 Creative Ways to Use Purpose, Prayer, and the Power of Spirit to Build a Meaningful Retirement
By Molly and Bernie Srode
As we face new demands on our bodies, it's easy to focus on the physical and forget about the transformations in our spiritual selves. This book is brimming with creative, practical ideas to add purpose and spirit to a meaningful retirement.
8 x 8, 224 pp, Quality PB, 978-1-59473-042-9 **$16.99**

Women's Interest

She Lives! Sophia Wisdom Works in the World
By Rev. Jann Aldredge-Clanton, PhD
Fascinating narratives of clergy and laypeople who are changing the institutional church and society by restoring biblical female divine names and images to Christian theology, worship symbolism and liturgical language.
6 x 9, 320 pp, Quality PB, 978-1-59473-573-8 **$18.99**

Birthing God: Women's Experiences of the Divine
By Lana Dalberg; Foreword by Kathe Schaaf
Powerful narratives of suffering, love and hope that inspire both personal and collective transformation. 6 x 9, 304 pp, Quality PB, 978-1-59473-480-9 **$18.99**

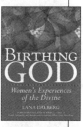

Women, Spirituality and Transformative Leadership
Where Grace Meets Power
Edited by Kathe Schaaf, Kay Lindahl, Kathleen S. Hurty, PhD, and Reverend Guo Cheen
A dynamic conversation on the power of women's spiritual leadership and its emerging patterns of transformation.
6 x 9, 288 pp, Quality PB, 978-1-59473-548-6 **$18.99**; HC, 978-1-59473-313-0 **$24.99**

Spiritually Healthy Divorce: Navigating Disruption with Insight & Hope
By Carolyne Call A spiritual map to help you move through the twists and turns of divorce. 6 x 9, 224 pp, Quality PB, 978-1-59473-288-1 **$16.99**

New Feminist Christianity: Many Voices, Many Views
Edited by Mary E. Hunt and Diann L. Neu
Insights from ministers and theologians, activists and leaders, artists and liturgists offer a starting point for building new models of religious life and worship.
6 x 9, 384 pp, Quality PB, 978-1-59473-435-9 **$19.99**; HC, 978-1-59473-285-0 **$24.99**

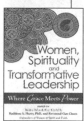

Bread, Body, Spirit: Finding the Sacred in Food
Edited and with Introductions by Alice Peck 6 x 9, 224 pp, Quality PB, 978-1-59473-242-3 **$19.99**

Dance—The Sacred Art: The Joy of Movement as a Spiritual Practice
By Cynthia Winton-Henry 5½ x 8½, 224 pp, Quality PB, 978-1-59473-268-3 **$16.99**

Daughters of the Desert: Stories of Remarkable Women from Christian, Jewish and Muslim Traditions *By Claire Rudolf Murphy, Meghan Nuttall Sayres, Mary Cronk Farrell, Sarah Conover and Betsy Wharton*
5½ x 8½, 192 pp, Illus., Quality PB, 978-1-59473-106-8 **$16.99** Inc. reader's discussion guide

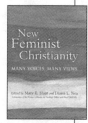

The Divine Feminine in Biblical Wisdom Literature
Selections Annotated & Explained
Translation & Annotation by Rabbi Rami Shapiro; Foreword by Rev. Cynthia Bourgeault, PhD
5½ x 8½, 240 pp, Quality PB, 978-1-59473-109-9 **$18.99**

Divining the Body: Reclaim the Holiness of Your Physical Self
By Jan Phillips 8 x 8, 256 pp, Quality PB, 978-1-59473-080-1 **$18.99**

Honoring Motherhood: Prayers, Ceremonies & Blessings
Edited and with Introductions by Lynn L. Caruso
5 x 7¼, 272 pp, Quality PB, 978-1-58743-384-0 **$9.99**; HC, 978-1-59473-239-3 **$19.99**

Next to Godliness: Finding the Sacred in Housekeeping
Edited by Alice Peck 6 x 9, 224 pp, Quality PB, 978-1-59473-214-0 **$19.99**

On the Chocolate Trail: A Delicious Adventure Connecting Jews, Religions, History, Travel, Rituals and Recipes to the Magic of Cacao *By Rabbi Deborah R. Prinz*
6 x 9, 272 pp, w/ 20+ b/w photographs, Quality PB, 978-1-58023-487-0 **$18.99***

The Triumph of Eve & Other Subversive Bible Tales
By Matt Biers-Ariel 5½ x 8½, 192 pp, Quality PB, 978-1-59473-176-1 **$14.99**

Woman Spirit Awakening in Nature: Growing Into the Fullness of Who You Are
By Nancy Barrett Chickerneo, PhD; Foreword by Eileen Fisher
8 x 8, 224 pp, b/w illus., Quality PB, 978-1-59473-250-8 **$16.99**

Women of Color Pray: Voices of Strength, Faith, Healing, Hope and Courage
Edited and with Introductions by Christal M. Jackson 5 x 7¼, 208 pp, Quality PB, 978-1-59473-077-1 **$15.99**

*A book from Jewish Lights, SkyLight Paths' sister imprint

Professional Spiritual & Pastoral Care Resources

Personal Growth

The Forgiveness Handbook
Spiritual Wisdom and Practice for the Journey to Freedom, Healing and Peace
Created by the Editors at SkyLight Paths; Introduction by The Rev. Canon Marianne Wells Borg
Offers inspiration, encouragement and spiritual practice from across faith traditions for all who seek hope, wholeness and the freedom that comes from true forgiveness. 6 x 9, 256 pp, Quality PB, 978-1-59473-577-6 **$18.99**

Decision Making & Spiritual Discernment: The Sacred Art of
Finding Your Way *By Nancy L. Bieber*
Presents three essential aspects of Spirit-led decision making: willingness, attentiveness and responsiveness.
5½ x 8½, 208 pp, Quality PB, 978-1-59473-289-8 **$16.99**

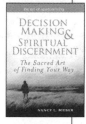

Like a Child
Restoring the Awe, Wonder, Joy and Resiliency of the Human Spirit
By Rev. Timothy J. Mooney
Explores Jesus's counsel to become like children in order to enter the kingdom of God. 6 x 9, 160 pp, Quality PB, 978-1-59473-543-1 **$16.99**

Secrets of a Soulful Marriage
Creating & Sustaining a Loving, Sacred Relationship
By Jim Sharon, EdD, and Ruth Sharon, MS
An innovative, hope-filled resource for developing soulful, mature love for committed couples who are looking to create, maintain and glorify the sacred in their relationship. Offers a banquet of practical tools, inspirational real-life stories and spiritual practices for couples of all faiths, or none.
6 x 9, 192 pp, Quality PB, 978-1-59473-554-7 **$16.99**

Hospitality—The Sacred Art
Discovering the Hidden Spiritual Power of Invitation and Welcome
By Rev. Nanette Sawyer; Foreword by Rev. Dirk Ficca
Discover how the qualities of hospitality can deepen your self-understanding and help you build transforming and lasting relationships with others and with God.
5½ x 8½, 208 pp, Quality PB, 978-1-59473-228-7 **$16.99**

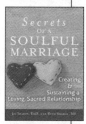

The Losses of Our Lives
The Sacred Gifts of Renewal in Everyday Loss
By Dr. Nancy Copeland-Payton
Shows us that by becoming aware of what our lesser losses have to teach us, the larger losses become less terrifying. Includes spiritual practices and questions for reflection.
6 x 9, 192 pp, Quality PB, 978-1-59473-307-9 **$16.99**; HC, 978-1-59473-271-3 **$19.99**

A Spirituality for Brokenness
Discovering Your Deepest Self in Difficult Times
By Terry Taylor
Compassionately guides you through the practicalities of facing and finally accepting brokenness in your life—a process that can ultimately bring mending.
6 x 9, 176 pp, Quality PB, 978-1-59473-229-4 **$16.99**

The Bridge to Forgiveness
Stories and Prayers for Finding God and Restoring Wholeness
By Karyn D. Kedar
Inspiring, deeply personal stories, comforting prayers and intimate meditations gently lead you through the steps that allow the heart to forgive.
6 x 9, 176 pp, Quality PB, 978-1-58023-451-1 **$16.99***

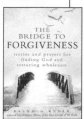

Conversation—The Sacred Art
Practicing Presence in an Age of Distraction
By Diane M. Millis, PhD; Foreword by Rev. Tilden Edwards, PhD
5½ x 8½, 192 pp, Quality PB, 978-1-59473-474-8 **$16.99**

*A book from Jewish Lights, SkyLight Paths' sister imprint

About SKYLIGHT PATHS Publishing

SkyLight Paths Publishing is creating a place where people of different spiritual traditions come together for challenge and inspiration, a place where we can help each other understand the mystery that lies at the heart of our existence.

Through spirituality, our religious beliefs are increasingly becoming a part of our lives—rather than *apart* from our lives. While many of us may be more interested than ever in spiritual growth, we may be less firmly planted in traditional religion. Yet, we do want to deepen our relationship to the sacred, to learn from our own as well as from other faith traditions, and to practice in new ways.

SkyLight Paths sees both believers and seekers as a community that increasingly transcends traditional boundaries of religion and denomination—people wanting to learn from each other, *walking together, finding the way.*

For your information and convenience, at the back of this book we have provided a list of other SkyLight Paths books you might find interesting and useful. They cover the following subjects:

Buddhism / Zen	Gnosticism	Poetry
Catholicism	Hinduism / Vedanta	Prayer
Chaplaincy		Religious Etiquette
Children's Books	Inspiration	Retirement & Later-Life Spirituality
Christianity	Islam / Sufism	
Comparative Religion	Judaism	Spiritual Biography
	Meditation	Spiritual Direction
Earth-Based Spirituality	Mindfulness	Spirituality
	Monasticism	Women's Interest
Enneagram	Mysticism	Worship
Global Spiritual Perspectives	Personal Growth	

Or phone, fax, mail or email to: SKYLIGHT PATHS Publishing
Sunset Farm Offices, Route 4 • P.O. Box 237 • Woodstock, Vermont 05091
Tel: (802) 457-4000 • Fax: (802) 457-4004 • www.skylightpaths.com
Credit card orders: (800) 962-4544 (8:30AM–5:30PM EST Monday–Friday)
Generous discounts on quantity orders. SATISFACTION GUARANTEED. Prices subject to change.